Golden Laurels, Silver Seas

Golden Laurels, Silver Seas

A Concise Survey of Greek History from the Bronze Age to the End of the Hellenistic Period

Aeon History

uxori liberisque

and

fratri parentibusque

Contents

Introduction

As the sun sinks behind the distant hills of Greece, you gaze across the bustling city of Athens. Leaning against a gigantic column of the Propylaea, the Acropolis' mighty gate, you imagine yourself standing there nearly 2,500 years ago. What had it looked like, unobscured by the veil of history?

Long ago, the groves of cypress, pine, and fir were thicker, filling the valley between the grey hills. Bracketed by outflung land, the Saronic Gulf's blue-grey waters lapped the shore, bringing ships from all over the world. Behind you, the Acropolis rose in the height of its glory with painted statues, garlanded pillars, and walkways thronged with philosophers and scholars. The whole world came to Greece.

Even today, you can almost feel their presence. The weight of the years has taken its toll on the Acropolis and other ancient Greek structures, but many columns still stand as a testament to the ancient Greeks who laid the foundations for Europe, and the modern world. Here, the first form of democracy arose, western philosophy began to inquire, and the residents helped draw political lines that would impact Europe and the Middle East for millennia.

Athens: The Birthplace of Western Culture

Ancient Greece. The name conjures up many images—philosophers, statues, crumbling stone monuments, and distant wars. Life in Ancient Greece was very different from what we are used to today. It was politically fragmented, with over 1,500 city-states dotting the mountainous landscape. Each of these city-states, called a *polis* by its inhabitants, had its own government and way of life, creating a diverse cultural landscape (National Geographic Society, 2022).

Athens, one of the larger *poleis*, was home to roughly 300,000 people during its height in the 5th century BCE. Compared to modern-day urban areas like Tokyo, Beijing, or Mexico City, that might not seem like a lot of people, but in ancient times, Athens was a major hub (Williams, 2008). Like Memphis, Babylon, and Rome, Athens was ground zero for major changes in the ancient world.

Some of these changes had long-term impacts on how we interact with each other today. The Greek alphabet evolved over time, was adapted, and finally used in most European languages. Using their language, ancient Greeks transformed academic knowledge, creating libraries, defining fields of study, and formulating theories that would be remembered for centuries.

Within this society, the fathers of philosophy, medicine, and history helped to create the frameworks of knowledge through which we still view the world. These scholars also preserved ancient tales, researched medicine, and synthesized common knowledge, which they spread to all corners of the ancient world.

Studying Ancient Greece, therefore, shows us where many of our fundamental presuppositions come from. Moreover, it allows us to understand how those ideas developed. We can learn why philosophical and political theories evolved, what life was like before the Golden Age of the Greek Empire, and how those changes still impact our world. In studying the decline of Ancient Greece, we can also gain perspective on the dynamics of nation and culture-building and what leads to the fragmentation of great empires.

Ancient Greece has a lot to teach us. Through the stories of its early history, the rise of its empire, and its eventual decline, we can learn about the people who transformed the world—both yesterday and today.

Voices of the Past

Biology. Geology. Mythology. Theology. All of these words are based on Ancient Greek. Their ending, "logy," comes from the Greek word "logos," which is related to ideas around reason, order, logic, and the power of words.

Interestingly, this word is linked to "lego," the Greek verb for "I speak" (*Logo-*, 2017). For the Ancient Greeks, the importance of one's voice was directly linked to the exercise of reason and logic. From these concepts arose a culture that transformed the world with new ideas of how to govern, organize society, and engage with culture.

Fast forward to the 21st century. In a world that views voting, personal property, and safety from predation as natural rights, Ancient Greece might feel like a whole other world. It's all too easy to lose the vitality and energy of the culture that *invented* the ideas we take for granted in a mountain of dates and names. History can become stale. In worst-case scenarios, it simply ends up a vehicle for our own perceptions and ideologies.

However, by exploring and experiencing the life and times of the Ancient Greeks with an open mind, we discover a complex, chaotic, and colorful world. But the Greeks talked about their experiences. They employed the power of the *logos*, revealed their hopes and dreams, and shared the challenges of their lives. Now, we can benefit from their wisdom.

Navigating Greek History

History helps us understand ourselves, gain perspective on our experiences, and find common ground with the people around us. Unfortunately, many present it as a slog. You probably know some important dates and names from school, but you might wonder, what's the point?

Golden Laurels, Silver Seas provides a concise, engaging, and accessible overview of Ancient Greece's history. Yet, it tries to balance these qualities with a comprehensive approach, covering all the most important elements of ancient Greek culture. Therefore, we believe it is a valuable resource for anyone interested in this fascinating period of history.

In this book, you will:

- discover engaging narratives told in chronological order with cultural insights, historical context, and important details.

- gain a comprehensive understanding of Ancient Greece's history, culture, politics, and contributions to the world.

- get to know the famous figures of Ancient Greece, from Homer to Herodotus, from Socrates to Aristotle, from Alexander the Great to Pericles.

- enjoy engaging and dramatic accounts of significant events like the Trojan War, the Battle of Thermopylae, and the death of Socrates.

- save time and effort by accessing all the important information about Ancient Greece in a concise, easy-to-read format.

We sincerely hope that *Golden Laurels, Silver Seas* will provide you with a comprehensive, easy-to-read introduction to Ancient Greece. Non-specialist readers of all levels should find it accessible, whether they are seasoned history buffs, or young newcomers to the heroic stories of Athens, Sparta, and many other Greek tales from the past.

Note: All translations from ancient sources are by Aeon History.

Part 1: Prehistory to the Bronze Age Collapse

Chapter 1: The Early Aegean

Across the silver sea and under blue skies filled with thin white clouds, a ship rollicks from one white-capped wave to another. The world seems a vast emptiness, dotted only by small rocky islands covered in gorse, grass, cypress, and pine. The ship pays no heed. They are moving northward to where the distant grey-green humps of the mountains beckon.

The men and women in this ship are from Crete, the largest of the Greek islands. They have come searching for new land. Dark-haired, dark-eyed, and gorgeously dressed in vibrant clothing, the Minoans (as we call them) represent the most advanced civilization in the region from the late 3rd to the early 2nd millennium BCE. Their remaining sculptures suggest that the women often wore floor-length gowns that fell in sectioned pleats, while their tops swooped to their waistline with plunging V-necks, revealing their breasts. The men, kilted and lightly armored, also wore cloaks and plumed helms.

During a time when civilizations hunkered down along the edges of mighty rivers, the Minoans were one of the few peoples to risk the intemperate seas. Their ships carried their culture throughout the Aegean and beyond. They produced artistic frescoes, elegant gold jewelry, finely crafted pottery, labyrinthine palaces, and enjoyed lively sports. Trade, religion, politics, and agriculture flourished under their care. The mysterious early civilizations of Crete and Greece laid the foundation for the future of Europe, and the rest of the world.

The Greek Landscape

Between North Africa and Europe, the Mediterranean Sea stretches. Toward the east, it meets the shores of modern-day Egypt, Israel, Syria, Lebanon, and Turkey. In that corner of the Mediterranean, to the northwest of Turkey, the Mediterranean Sea opens into a smaller sea that spreads between Greece and Turkey. This is the Aegean, dotted with the beautiful islands of Santorini, Rhodes, Chios, and Naxos.

General groupings can help to visualize island locations a bit easier. The Ionian Islands sit in the Ionian Sea, to the west of mainland Greece. The Aegean Sea is home to the Saronic, the Sporades, the Cyclades, and the Dodecanese island groups.

The Saronic Islands are wedged between Athens and the east coast of the Peloponnese. The Sporades hug the eastern coast of mainland Greece north of Euboea. The Cyclades are particularly important for early Greek culture and dwell in the center of the Aegean to the north of Crete. Finally, the Dodecanese Islands stretch southeast toward modern Turkey, culminating in Rhodes, the largest of the group.

Looking more closely at the Greek mainland, we see that it is a peninsula: to the east, the Aegean Sea;

to the south, the Mediterranean; to the west, the Ionian.

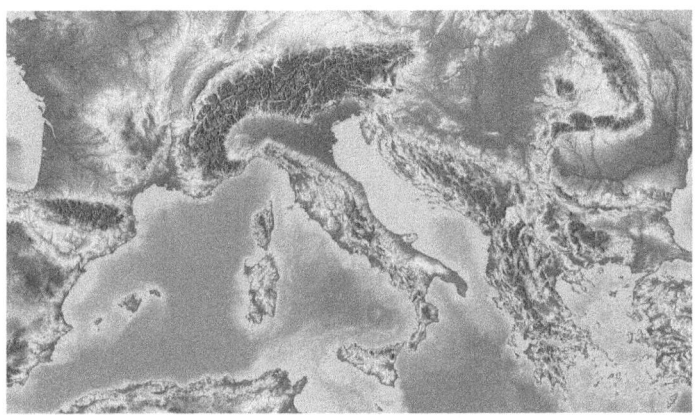

Down the middle of this peninsula runs the massive Pindus Mountain range, the lower reaches of the larger Dinaric Alps of the Balkans. Other mountain ranges are found in the northeast of Greece, such as the Voras Mountains. The Peloponnese Peninsula also has its own Taygetus Mountain range. The tallest of the mountains, Mount Olympus, reaches an elevation of just under 9,500 feet. Remote and majestic, Mount Olympus became connected with the realm of the gods (Ancient Greece Geography: Landscape & Map, 2023).

At lower altitudes, however, Greece remains firmly in the realm of men. The slopes, hills, and sheltered plains allow for olive trees, forests, and green land suitable for farming and herding. In the south of Greece, its clement Mediterranean weather means that winters are not very cold (rather, they are rainy), while the summers are hot and dry. In the north, winter feels colder, and snow falls. This variable climate encourages considerable biodiversity in a relatively small geographic area.

After taking all that Crete had to offer, early peoples looked to the north, to Greece, for more land and resources. Fertile valleys became a comfortable home for the early Bronze Age farmers. Crops of grapes, lentils, cabbage, onion, beans, and garlic were plentiful. Fruit and nut trees, like apples, almonds, pears, and figs, were also common. On top of that, savory herbs were also encouraged to grow—sage, mint, and thyme, among others.

Livestock could thrive as well, feasting on the plenteous greenery. Sheep and goats were capable of moving through mountainous terrain, so many ancient Greeks were sheepherders. Other, smaller domestic animals like pigs were common, but cattle were a bit rarer. These livestock provided early Greeks with milk and meat, and one day would become a source of cheese, wool, and leather. Horses, donkeys, and mules were used for transportation.

However, since Greece consisted of large mountain ranges and a widely spread archipelago, it was difficult for its earliest inhabitants to connect their communities into a cohesive whole. Many villages were isolated. Early Greeks who explored for more land and resources in modern-day southern Italy, Turkey, and North Africa were even less connected with the other ancient Greek towns. As a result, each settlement began to form its own culture, laws, and dialects. The birth of the *polis*, the city-state, had begun.

Early Civilization

As far back as the Stone and Bronze Ages, civilization has flourished in Greece and the islands of the Aegean. Over 2.5 million years ago, during the Paleolithic, or Old Stone Age, early humans began to slowly develop tools and early forms of culture. The Neolithic, New Stone Age, generally dated to 7,000–3,000 B.C.E., especially marked a period characterized by simple yet important advancements.

As suggested by the name, tools during this period were made of stone, and agriculture was basic. There are hints that religion and rudimentary culture were present, as well. Thanks to the remaining clay figurines of animals and women at burial sites and sanctuaries, we understand that society was beginning to form at this early stage.

The New Stone Age

Findings on a small island called Melos near Crete show that small boats were in use throughout the Neolithic. These early sailors were scavenging and collecting obsidian for toolmaking, and they were already farming basic grain, domesticating animals, and fishing for tuna. However, thanks to the climate and fertile lands in the area, more technological advancements were made, and humans began to spread throughout the region.

The great advance of the Neolithic was agriculture, and it spread from the Middle East to the Greek islands. Pottery was developed, and the art of firing ceramic vases began to allow for increased development in cooking. At the same time, new tools began to spring up—axes, chisels, and grinding stones. Agricultural crops expanded to oats, lentils, peas, and fruit. Arrowheads dug up in mainland Greece and the Cyclades point to the use of archery. Slings and clubs were used in other areas of the world at the time, including Egypt, so it is believed that these were also probably common.

By this point in time, communities were more settled. At Knossos on Crete as well as at other sites in the Cyclades and in Macedonia, archaeologists discovered ancient sites of Late Neolithic communities. Houses were made of stone, although they were simple rectangles or circular structures. More houses were built next to each other, forming the first acropolis towns; some towns had walls and up to 30 houses. Late Neolithic communities also boasted megarons, which were large central halls, as can be seen at Dhimini, in northern Greece.

With this growth, culture began to once again flourish. Pottery became more complex with patterns of various colors. Social hierarchies began to form, and dominant chiefs led their communities. However, civilization wasn't finished progressing yet. A

new era dawned—the Bronze Age (Townsend Vermeule & Hood, 1999).

The Bronze Age

The Bronze Age is usually dated from roughly
3,000–1,000 B.C.E. As more people traveled west-
ward from the Mesopotamian cradle of civilization,
they brought innovations in working with metals.
Tools began to transform again as the people of ancient Greece learned how to use copper, bronze, and
other metals.

However, since they were more isolated, the Cycladic settlements in the Aegean archipelago
developed later. As a result, three cultures arose with
many similarities but some distinctive differences—
the Cycladic, the Helladic, and a Cretan civilization
that would develop into the Minoans of this chapter's
introduction.

Cycladic Civilization

The Cycladic culture flourished in the islands of
the Aegean to the east of mainland Greece. Although
their isolation resulted in some lags in advancement,
these people shared many characteristics with other
Bronze Age groups. Nevertheless, they were already
defining their cultic practices. Family cemeteries began to spring up. White marble sculptures were
carved, and stone vases were regularly created. White
marble was particularly popular, so these islands had

regular exports they could send to the mainland or to Crete.

Toward the middle of the Bronze Age, Cretans began to form definitive colonies on the island of Cythera as well as on Rhodes and in Anatolia, modern Turkey. While the two peoples seemed to coexist fairly peacefully, the original inhabitants of the Cyclades only borrowed pieces of Cretan culture. They maintained their own identity, as can be seen from the artifacts left behind.

During this period, pottery was decorated with flowers and animals, including depictions of bluebirds and dolphins. Frescoes, pictures of animals and fishermen, were discovered on the island of Thera. Paintings show that life, like many cultures around the world, involved a mixture of tranquil civilization and war (Townsend Vermeule & Hood, 1999).

Helladic Civilization

At the same time, the Helladic civilization flourished on the mainland. As in the Cyclades islands, houses became more complex and permanent. Towns began to grow. They began to add balconies to houses, and innovations in roofing led to the first creation of tiles in the region.

With a growth in population, early forms of government began to develop. Religious and cultural rituals became more complex. While burials on the mainland are less well-known, excavations reveal that mainland graves contained several bodies at a time, usually from close-knit families. Many of these tombs were cut into rocks or covered with heaps of stones, called cairns.

At Lerna, a Greek city, archaeological digs reveal that invaders entered the region from the middle of the Bronze Age onwards. After destroying the native settlements, rebuilding wasn't easy, resulting in more primitive housing. These new groups, who might have come from the Balkans or the Black Sea, brought new pottery, rituals, and ornamentation. They were likely the ones who introduced horses to Greece. The pottery was darker, and some of it had linear patterns, suggesting that the invaders shared some affinities with the culture they conquered.

Minoan Civilization

Throughout the Bronze Age, Cretan civilization also developed rapidly. Unlike the more distant communities on Greece's mainland and its islands, Crete had direct connections to Egypt and the Middle East. As a result, it developed alongside its neighbors, creating larger cities, hierarchal social structures, elaborate rituals, and beautiful art. However, the true flower of Cretan civilization would come to a head with the Minoan civilization. The Minoans were about to change the world (Townsend Vermeule & Hood, 1999).

Shrouded in myths, the start of the Minoan civilization begins with a tale of a mighty king. The legendary King Minos appears in myth as the son of

Zeus. He is also linked to other deities and supernatural beasts, including the minotaur, a half-man, half-bull figure.

However, ancient historians like Thucydides and recent excavations in Crete suggest that Minos probably did exist, in a sense. The name "Minos" was probably a kind of title, similar to "President" or "King," used for rulers who also fulfilled religious functions.

There were other mysterious religious figures like the Snake Goddess, a gowned woman wearing the Cretan-styled bare-chested top while clutching snakes. Was this a unique goddess, or did this represent a special order of priestesses known to Crete? To this day, no one is certain (German, 2022). What *is* known is that the legends surrounding bulls and snakes evolved into complex cultural rituals. From the worship of bulls came fascinating sports, including bull-jumping, where athletes would jump through the wide horns of a bull as a show of flexibility and courage.

According to Thucydides, the first King Minos expanded Cretan territory to the Cyclades islands. He expelled the original settlers and began to govern a growing empire of pirates. The Cretan's thalassocracy, a word which translates from the Greek as "sea power," wasn't focused on warfare. His goal was to trade, as evidenced by the number of Cretan artifacts discovered at sites around the Mediterranean.

From the palace in Knossos, the kings of Crete dominated trade in the Aegean Sea. They sent timber, wool, ceramics, and bronze vessels to Egypt, and sent daggers, lamps, and stone and bronze vessels to Cyprus. Italy and the northern lands around the Aegean Sea imported a variety of these Cretan products.

Thanks to the advancements and efficient production of the Minoans, their civilization lasted from around 3,000–1,100 B.C.E. Its art, architecture, tools, and rituals became more complex over time. Larger public buildings in Knossos were painted with gorgeous frescoes depicting religious, mythological, or everyday life scenes. Beyond art, the palace showcased higher advancements in city building and maintenance. The streets were paved, and water was brought to the palace in pipes.

Some archaeologists believe these "palaces" were more like central distribution hubs for the islanders.

Most of the people lived in stone, wood, or brick houses, living off the land as farmers, lumberjacks, or artisans. Goldsmithing was one of the highlights of Cretan creativity. Since the Minoans were spread across the island, even larger hubs like Knossos did not raise thick city walls. Their wall was the Mediterranean Sea. Any who approached shore would easily be picked off by experienced Minoan sailors.

Since Crete was isolated but not too distant from larger nations, it was able to maintain independence for a while. Its navy, considered by later historians to be the first of its kind, colonized the Cyclades islands and spread to other corners of the Mediterranean Sea for trade. From this foundational civilization, Greece was given the knowledge of complex city construction, shipbuilding, and other forms of engineering. Studying the Minoans, they clearly impacted the world around them, but there is still so much we don't know (Movellán Luis, 2018).

Early Writing in Greece

The main reason why archaeologists and historians struggle to decipher the details of Minoan culture is because its language remains a mystery. The first two widespread writing systems to appear in Greece are called Linear A and Linear B. While Linear B has been deciphered, Linear A remains a mystery. What is known is that both languages have been found on thousands of clay tablets and pottery, representing two distinct periods.

In the center and south of Crete, scholars have found many samples of Linear A. Its epicenter was Crete, between 1,900–1,500 B.C.E., though examples have been found on other Aegean islands, mainland Greece, and Anatolia. It was the common writing system used before the arrival of the Mycenaean Greeks.

Another hieroglyphic script was found in the north and eastern areas of Crete. There is debate about whether the two are related or not. To make matters even more confusing, a third script was also discovered by Italian archaeologist Luigi Pernier in 1908 on a famous artifact called the Phaistos Disk.

A few observations have been made about Linear A. Scholars surmise it comprises at least three vowels and around 90 common symbols. Like many Western writing systems, it reads left to right and top to bottom, in rows. The writing symbol is more abstract than Egyptian hieroglyphics and is drawn with lines, giving it the name Linear A (Hirst, 2018).

However, the difficulty in translation is that there is no obvious key. While there are many examples of Linear A, no Rosetta Stone-like translation has been found. Another problem is that Linear A texts are mostly just lists of words, not full sentences, which means that it isn't as easy to crack as many other languages.

Additionally, Linear A is an early representation of language writing systems built on syllables, like modern-day Japanese or Cherokee. When Linear B was deciphered, it helped identify some things, such as which symbol represented which sound. However, it can't tell what the sounds combined mean.

Overall, Linear B has proven less of a puzzle. Studies of the writing system prove it was borrowed from the Minoans around 1,600 B.C.E. and co-opted by the Mycenaeans, who had settled in southern Greece by about 1750 B.C.E. It was deciphered in the 1950s, and is considered to be the Mycenaean civilization's major writing system, representing their archaic dialect of the Greek language (Hirst, 2018).

In 2023, linguist Dr. Ester Salgarella pioneered new translation techniques to definitively prove the link between the two writing systems. Drawing on linguistics, archaeology, and paleography techniques, as well as a digital database, Dr. Salgarella was able to analyze the mysterious Linear A in detail. Salgarella hoped to provide a foundation for future linguists to work from, clarifying the symbols used and ensuring that no misclassification of signs would happen.

At the same time, Salgarella realized that both writing systems are directly linked. After a sharp decline of Minoan civilization shortly after 1500 B.C.E., there was a 50-year gap where no writing seemed to happen. During this period, there was a switch, where the writing more or less remained familiar, but the actual language it represented dramatically changed. The closest comparison today might be the difference between Cantonese and Mandarin Chinese, languages that share similar writing systems but whose pronunciation is different and whose underlying languages are not mutually intelligible (Claus, 2023).

There is a lot of work to be done. With the number of Linear A's symbols, it may never be fully decipherable. However, what linguists are able to guess is that the Minoan civilization thoroughly dedicated to record keeping, a testament to their mercantile tendencies. Their language system would inspire other people's writing and evolve into the Greek alphabet we are familiar with today—the origin of the Latin alphabet that is so influential in the modern world.

The Timeless Impact of Crete

We may never hear the voices of the Minoan civilization; their words are locked behind coded messages. Their myths and rituals may have been lost to time, and their enigmatic figures, like the Snake Goddess, may never be fully understood. One thing is for certain, however—the impact of their advancements on the early settlers of Greece. Not only did they help usher in a new age of metalwork, but they also diversified the world around them through their trade.

Between 1,500 and 1,400 B.C.E., the Minoan culture fell into sharp decline. A century is a long time to experience in person, but, in archaeological terms, it is almost like the Minoans disappeared overnight. Why? No one is certain.

Some posit that a volcano on Santorini disrupted the area, leading to earthquakes and potential tsunamis. Others suggest that signs of fire and desecration at the Knossos ruins point to marauders. Either way, the ancient city of Knossos fell, and Crete lost its grip on the Mediterranean Sea. Yet, in a way, their story was not over.

From the hands of the Minoans came knowledge and tools that empowered the next civilization—the Mycenaeans. Known for fortified palaces and military prowess, this new group dominated the Greek landscape for centuries, playing a central role in one of the most-remembered myths of antiquity—the Trojan War. In the next chapter, we will explore the rise of the Mycenaean civilization and the world of heroes and legends it left behind.

Chapter 2: The Mycenaean Age

"Goddess, sing the wrath of Peleus' son Achilles,
destructive, that brought boundless suffering to the Achaeans.
For it sent to Hades many stouthearted souls
of heroes, and made their corpses carrion for all manner
of dogs and birds. Thus was the will of Zeus fulfilled."
(Homer, *Iliad*, 1.1-5)

This is a tale of desperate men, besieging one of the largest cities of antiquity—Troy. The famous warriors Achilles, Hector, Paris, and Odysseus clashed blades, leading armies in an epic siege. Pushed to the edge, the Greek army of King Agamemnon was faced with two choices: return home in disgrace, or risk everything to take the city.

Odysseus hatched a plan: Build a large hollow horse and pack it with the surviving heroes of the Greek army. Hopefully, the city would open its gates and bring it in. Despite the warnings of some Trojans, Odysseus's plan succeeded. With the help of one "survivor" who spun a tale, the Trojan people welcomed the gift and dragged the horse into the city. The rest is history. Sort of.

The historicity of the Trojan War remained unquestioned throughout antiquity and the Middle Ages. However, by the end of the Renaissance, the stories of Troy were considered myths. Nevertheless, archaeological data over the decades has filled in the gaps, bringing to light more information about the civilization that rose to dominance after the Minoan's decline.

The Mycenaeans were warriors, architects, and traders who left an indelible mark on Greek history and mythology. They dominated the late Bronze Age in Greece, and they played a central role in one of the most famous (hi)stories ever told—the Trojan War.

Rise of the Mycenaeans

Partially overlapping the Minoan culture, the Mycenaeans flourished in mainland Greece from 1,600–1,100 B.C.E. Although they stuck to the mountains and valleys of the peninsula, the Mycenaeans mingled with visiting Minoans. And even as the Minoan civilization precipitously declined after about 1450 B.C.E., the Mycenaeans persevered. They adapted the Minoan writing system to fit their needs and continued to develop the tools and advancements that the Minoans had introduced.

How closely related were the Mycenaeans to the Minoans? After extracting and analyzing DNA from 19 individuals, researchers discovered that the Minoans and Mycenaeans were, in fact, genetically related. They appear to have both come from Anatolia.

Furthermore, although the Minoan culture disappeared, significant traces of Bronze Age DNA (both Minoan and Mycenaean) have persisted in modern-day Greeks (*Ancient DNA Reveals Origins of the Minoans and Mycenaeans*, n.d.). However, the Mycenaeans didn't just impact the gene pool. They also helped to define Greek culture with their political organization and cultural development.

Although many people place the Mycenaean civilization after the Minoan, the truth is that the Mycenaeans were around for quite some time. For 150 years, between 1,600–1,450 B.C.E., the two civilizations flourished concurrently. It was only in the final 350 to 450 years of the Bronze Age that the Minoans fell into decline, allowing the Mycenaeans to take center stage. Some scholars even suggest it was the Mycenaeans who conquered the Minoans.

Either way, what is certain is that Mycenae began to dominate the Mediterranean Sea in matters of trade. They picked up where the Minoans left off, selling pottery and other articles to Egypt, Sicily, and the Mesopotamian civilizations. Like the Minoans, they also assumed ownership of the Cycladic islands.

At the same time, the Mycenaeans were very observant. Just as they learned from the Minoans, so they also learned from other neighboring civilizations. This allowed them to flourish for almost 500 years (Greek Boston, 2017).

Spreading across the Aegean Sea and the peninsula, the Mycenaeans built cities, including Mycenae, Pylos, Thebes, Argos, Athens, and Sparta. Mycenae, their largest city, was built on a high hill around 900 feet above sea level. On top of this hill, they built a massive citadel complete with walls, tombs, and large, palace-like buildings. Another important city linked to Mycenae is Athens. Some scholars believe that modern-day Greece's capital was originally a Mycenaean fortress.

The Mycenaeans didn't just settle the peninsula and the Cycladic islands. Relying on the naval advancements of the Minoans, they traveled further afield, eventually re-settling Crete and rebuilding Knossos. In this way, the fledgling civilization began to truly make an impact on the cultural landscape of the Aegean Sea (Cartwright, 2019).

Daily Life in Mycenae

What was life like in Mycenae and its far-flung outposts of hilltop citadels? Thanks to archaeological discovery and research, we are able to piece together a picture of Mycenae's vibrant culture. This was a tough, hard-working people who plied their trade around the Mediterranean.

With the flow of goods and wealth, farming and the domestication of animals continued, tools and weapons were developed further, settlements were able to solidify, and faith and political organization were codified. Their daily lives, marked by an increase in wealth and luxury commodities, were comfortable. The Mycenaeans might have been a profoundly warlike civilization, but the late Greek Bronze Age was a time of abundance.

Technological Innovations and Advancements

The greatest advancements heralded by the Mycenaeans were the formalization of monumental architecture like palaces and tholos tombs, the development of ceramics, and the evolution of Linear B script. Of course, the Minoans' influence continued to impact the Mycenaean people's production, but the Mycenaeans were invested in improving what they already knew.

The Mycenaeans improved architecture and defined how later Greek states would envision the building of structures. The Minoans had large cultural centers, to be sure. However, the more war-like Mycenaeans invested time and money to develop new types of walls, palaces, and fortified buildings in major cities like Mycenae, Thebes, and Tiryns. In these ancient ruins, you will find massive stone blocks placed to form thick walls, corbel-arched doorways, and large palace complexes.

Also, Mycenaean dig sites reveal that the civilization improved pottery and ceramic production. For as long as humans have eaten, they have also had to develop ways to store food. In Mycenae, ceramic production increased in innovation and intricacy. Pots like the "Warrior Krater" that have been dug up reveal that some were quite large and richly decorated with pictures of people or scenes of daily life.

Finally, the Mycenaeans appear to have adapted Linear A, the Minoans' writing system, to their dialect of Greek, producing Linear B. They preserved the

Minoan tendency to keep meticulous records, but they also put writing on some of their pottery. This became one of the hallmarks of what we recognize today as Classical Greek pottery (Stirn, 2022).

Religion and Politics

Thanks to the development of agriculture and trade, humans had now been settled for quite some time. As populations grouped together to form larger settlements, society became more organized, hierarchical, and stable. Concepts like family lineage and class were now considered the norm.

Upper-class Mycenaeans would take part in military, religious, or political affairs. The lower class was more involved in trade, production, and farming. During this period of time, slavery also existed, and the lower classes, as well as women, were allotted fewer rights and privileges.

The Mycenaeans may not have had computers, the Internet, or cameras, but they were still involved in running governments, creating bureaucratic structures, and keeping records. Excavations of Mycenae have revealed that bureaucracy played a key role in Mycenaean daily life as well as in war.

From tablets and death masks, we now know that the head of each settlement was called the wanax. Ruling from a massive palace, the wanax was considered a priest-king who ruled over the city and its surrounding land. Other classes identified in Mycenaean culture include:

- ***lawagetas***: leaders or administrators

- ***heqetai***: aristocratic warriors

- ***telestas***: landowners

- ***demos***: common classes (artisans and tradesmen)

- ***doeri***: slaves and women

Perpetuating the common social hierarchies of their times, the Mycenaeans preferred to give importance to their wealthy aristocratic warriors and landowners. This social structure would persist for millennia (Roberts, 2023).

Archaeologists have also identified traces of structured religion during this period. In tombs, golden masks highlighted important figures, such as the *wanax*. Jewelry, swords, and crowns also reveal the beautiful craftsmanship of the Mycenaean people. Frescoes depict the Mycenaeans sacrificing animals on alters, enjoying feasts together, offering food, and pouring libations (wine or other liquids) to the gods. Carrying forward many Minoan ideas, the symbol of the bull persisted (Klaeser, 2021).

Life and Culture

During this period, art, fashion, and cultural activities flourished. In frescoes, jewelry, and pottery, we can see how the Mycenaean artisans enjoyed using geometric or decorative patterns like spirals, rosettes, and lines. Homes were decorated with sculptures, paintings, and figurines that hint at common scenes of daily life—boar hunts, bull leaping, and battle scenes.

Fashion and clothing at this time reflected Minoan influence. The women still wore floor-length gowns that were often tiered in multicolored flounces. Sometimes they would cover their plunging necklines with a thin bodice.

Men's fashion changed more drastically. Instead of wearing just a loin cloth and helmet, Mycenaean men began to wear boat-necked tunics that fell to their thighs or knees. This style would set a fashion trend that would last millennia (*What Did They Wear in Ancient Greece? Mycenaean Attire*, n.d.).

Trade

When the massive trading empire of the Minoans fell into ruin, the Mycenaeans stepped in and took over. Not only did they continue to trade with the isolated communities found among the islands of the Aegean Sea and the shores of Turkey, but they continued to ferry their wares to Sicily, Cyprus, and other nations and empires in the Middle East. In the ruins of these ancient civilizations, Mycenaean artifacts have been found—gold, glass, copper, and ivory. Other important exports included wine, olive oil, and perfume.

In order to produce special wares, the Mycenaean people had to import exotic goods. While there aren't a lot of Linear B records to read, archaeologists found other ways to figure out what these new traders ferried around the Mediterranean Sea. A shipwreck off the coast of Turkey tells a fascinating tale. It sank sometime during the 1300s B.C.E. Its hold carried raw materials that would have been turned into specialty items, such as ivory, glass disks, tin ingots, and copper. All of these discoveries point to a time of bustling activity, commercial life, and creative expression (Cartwright, 2019).

Mycenaean Architecture

With social and political organization as well as relative economic and agricultural stability, the Mycenaeans were able to focus on other ways to express themselves creatively, take part in rituals, or highlight their social standing. One of the most fascinating legacies of Mycenae and its sister fortresses was its architectural achievements. The walls, *tholos* tombs, and *megarons* have defined Greek notions of beauty, stateliness, and power for millennia.

As migrants or invaders themselves, Mycenaeans understood the importance of a good wall. Unlike the Minoans who did not employ fortification walls

around their civic centers and palaces, the Mycenaean civilization wanted to keep new invaders out.
One such type of wall, known as the Cyclopean wall,
helped to protect Mycenaean interests.

In Mycenae, Thebes, and Tiryns, remnants of Cyclopean walls can still be seen today. Named after the
giant Cyclops of mythology, the unworked blocks that
made up these walls were so huge that it was said (by
later Greeks) that only a Cyclops could lift them.
Reaching to heights of 42 feet and widths of up to 26
feet, these walls were incredibly thick. They marked

an increased interest in security and allowed the Mycenaeans to live in relative security during a time when other empires began to expand (Cartwright, 2019).

Besides building walls, Mycenaeans began to evolve their burial rituals. At first, they used shaft graves, dug into the rock, where they placed their dead with important belongings at the bottom of a vertical shaft that would then be filled in with rubble and dirt. Some shaft graves were dug close together in circles, signifying kinships. Later on, however, horizontal tombs cut into rock and family sepulchers were built. These circular vaults, called *tholos* (plural: *tholoi*) tombs, were cut into hills and accessed by an arched door.

The largest of the tholoi are impressive, even today. The tholos at Mycenae called the "Treasury of Atreus" is around 50 feet in diameter and almost as high. The lintel of the doorway is an enormous monolith weighing 120 tons. The central circular room was used to house the tombs and later to conduct rituals. Even after the people connected to the dead were long gone, others would return to tholoi to continue rituals for hero-based worship (Hoffmann, 2000).

Mycenaeans also organized social and political spaces clearly. Their permanent settlements included massive palace structures for the *wanax* and society's elite, which followed common patterns. In the center of the palace, a large rectangular central hall, the *megaron*, would be erected to hold the *wanax*'s court.

Each megaron would have an entrance porch, a foyer or vestibule, and then the hall itself. In the center of the main hall, a round hearth surrounded by columns would be set into the floor, while above it a hole in the ceiling allowed for ventilation. The megaron would also have smaller versions for the queen as well as a host of side rooms for work, storage, and daily life activities.

A symbol of power and authority, the megaron's walls were limestone blocks covered with plaster; its ceilings were vaulted with wood and bronze. Painted with frescoes and other decorative motifs, the palace complexes spoke to a wealthy and artistic civilization.

Later in history, the Archaic and Classical Greeks would look to these forms for inspiration, and the Mycenaean palaces would become templates for Greek halls and temples. The power and art of the Mycenaean civilization would live on (Cartwright, 2019).

The Trojan War

The Mycenaens also left for posterity one other important thing—their stories. Classical and later Greeks didn't question the historicity of the Trojan War, neither did the Romans or Medieval Europeans. But belief in the veracity of heroic tales about the war waned by the 19th century AD. For a long time, the story seemed implausible. Did it really happen? Or was it just some kind of folk hero tale, epic saga, or myth-inspired text?

Although there were many texts describing the events of the Trojan War, including Homer's famous works, the *Iliad* and the *Odyssey*, as well as Virgil's *Aeneid*, many scholars doubted that the events of these epic tales were real. Homer wrote in the 8th century B.C.E., 400 years after the events of the Trojan War, while Virgil, a Roman poet, lived much later, from 70 to 19 B.C.E., more than 1,000 years after the war. As a result, many scholars doubted the truth of their tales. Then, Heinrich Schliemann, a German archaeologist, revealed a massive discovery in the late 1800s—the fabled city of Troy.

The Story of Troy

The story of Troy, as told by Homer, was fantastical. There were gods, goddesses, handsome warriors, and beautiful queens. There was drama, manipulation, intrigue, and death. Homer and Virgil's writings depicted convoluted plots, highlighted ancient places, and described a war between two peoples. On one side were the Greeks, led by King Agamemnon of Mycenae and his brother King Menelaus of Sparta; on the other, the people of Troy, led by King Priam, and his sons Hector and Paris.

The siege of Troy lasted 10 years and resulted in many deaths on both sides. According to Homer and Virgil, Troy eventually fell due to cunning strategy and deceit. The Greeks, packed into a hollow horse, were dragged into the city. At nightfall, they emerged to lay the great city of Troy to waste.

While the stories of the Trojan War sound exciting, it was a matter of debate over centuries of scholarship. To begin with, the active presence of gods, like Poseidon, Athena, Aphrodite, and Zeus, sets the epic poems directly in the realm of myth. Furthermore, the famous people mentioned, like King Agamemnon and King Priam, hadn't been found in any ancient burial site.

Also, Homer's Iliad only focused on a short period near the end of the 10-year war. The Odyssey, set after the Trojan War, chronicled the return of Odysseus to his family home. Neither appeared to have been written with historicity in mind. As a result, scholars weren't certain whether to treat the stories about Troy as fact. It wouldn't be until the late 1800s that Troy was definitively identified.

Discovering Troy

In 1870, Heinrich Schliemann led a group of archaeologists at a dig site at Hissarlik in western Turkey on the shores of the Aegean Sea. As the team dug deeper, they began to reveal older layers of history. The layers revealed a pattern of settlement, wherein a city was abandoned, then new settlers would arrive at the ruins, fill them in, and then build on top. The process created what is known as a mound, or "tell." There was about 80 feet of debris to sift through in some places, but the team managed to locate Bronze Age ruins far below.

Over 46 buildings were uncovered. Further excavations revealed that a city 10 times larger than the citadel surrounded the central ruins that were uncovered. Was this Troy?

Schliemann's hunch may have been correct. The site's origins were dated as far back as 3,000 B.C.E. Signs suggested that one of the largest layers had been abandoned around 1,100 B.C.E., around the time later Greeks believed the war to have taken place.

If the poets and local lore about the dating of the Trojan War were correct, it would place this site as a reasonable location for Troy. What was clear was that during Homer's time in the 8th century, the city's ruins would have been visible, kindling the imagination of one of history's greatest poetic traditions. Over time, it was covered in debris, waiting for Schliemann to stumble across it (History.com Editors, 2023).

For some people, the site of Troy might not look particularly exciting. The statuary is in bad shape, weathered by wind and destructive human force. Many walls are intact, but beyond a few small areas, no vaulted palaces remain. Paving stones are cracked with grass, and only a few pieces are inscribed with ancient lettering. However, for scholars, the discovery of Troy rocked the world.

The idea that there had been many versions of Troy helped cement the concept of borrowed settlements and mounds, where later inhabitants would move in or build on top of older structures. It also allowed archaeologists and historians to properly study the permutations of Anatolian and Greek civilizations. It was clear that later Greek, Anatolian, Middle Eastern, and Roman populations revered the site as the fabled city. King Xerxes and Alexander the Great personally visited the area. Later on, Romans would go on pilgrimages to visit the place where Aeneas, the ancestor of Romulus and Remus, had started his own epic adventure.

Finally, the site of Troy was able to reveal what challenges the people of that time faced. Scholars were able to make some guesses as to what really brought about the fall of Troy—earthquakes and political conflict (Jarus, 2017).

The Significance of Mycenae

Given how distant the Mycenaean civilization lies in the past, the fact it had a massive long-term impact on Greece might sound extreme. However, by continuing to pursue the Minoans' trading, writing system, and commercial practices, the Mycenaeans were able to nurture the growth of human civilization in the Aegean. Their willingness to communicate with and learn from neighboring cultures allowed them to flourish.

In this way, their stories, later preserved by oral traditions, became the myths that later Greek culture wrote down. Furthermore, by preserving the budding system of coherent small urban centers, the Mycenaeans set the stage for political drama for centuries to come.

On top of that, we can see how the Mycenaeans perpetuated increasingly complex architecture and agricultural techniques. Their walls, agricultural terraces, gates, and bridges signaled the arrival of more established public spaces. Mycenaean architectural innovations would inspire Greek religious, civic, and military structures for millennia.

The Mycenaeans were one of the great Bronze Age civilizations, but even so, they would fall into dark times. When the Mycenaean Age came to an end, Greece entered a period of decline known as the Greek Dark Ages.

It was a time of cultural regression, but it also set the stage for the emergence of the Classical Greek civilization that would follow. In the next chapter, we'll explore the Greek Dark Ages and how they shaped the world of ancient Greece.

Chapter 3: The Bronze Age Collapse and Greek Dark Ages

A weathered shepherd whistles tunelessly as he follows his small flock of sheep along a narrow, dusty path. The sun is sinking behind the now-shadowed mountains. As he moves quickly down the path, making his way home, his gaze rests on ancient ruins rising on the hill.

Long ago, it was said, they had housed kings and warriors. Heroes had fought armies, and the gods themselves came down to meddle in the affairs of men. The shepherd shivers. But that's all they are, he reminds himself. Tales. There are no more heroes, kings, epic battles, or visits from gods. Greece is abandoned. Its darkest days have arrived.

After the fall of the Mycenaean civilization, Greece plunged into centuries of obscurity and silence—an age so dark that it would forever be enshrouded in myths, legends, and unanswered questions. From about 1,150–800 B.C.E., Greece experienced a difficult transition into the Iron Age. Trade contracted, and many of the advancements of the Minoans and Mycenaeans would be forgotten. Some, for a time. Others, forever. Most importantly, writing ceased.

During this period, the Greeks lost their social structures as their political leaders were removed, their population decreased, and their survival threatened. Culture-making was put on hold. But how did this happen? What caused such a drastic shift? The mystery only deepens (Mark, 2015).

The Dorian Invasion

Beginning with the advancements of the Minoan culture and iterating on what they had learned from their many neighbors, the Mycenaeans should have continued their upward trend, conquering new lands, establishing new trade routes, improving their military, and shoring up their defenses. However, for some unknown reason, the civilization collapsed over a period of about 200 years, from 1,200 to 1,000 B.C.E. For many scholars, the reasons for the decline of the Mycenaean culture are still not certain. One strong theory emerged—the Dorian Invasion.

The Causes and Effects of Collapse

What exactly happened to the Mycenaeans? Several theories have been suggested, ranging from climate change to natural disasters to direct human intervention.

Climate change has been a long-term factor in history-making. Difficult living conditions, such as an ice age or increased temperatures, can result in human migration. According to anthropologists and climate scientists, the Mediterranean Sea underwent a rapid cooling phase around 1,100 B.C.E. Consequently, less rain fell. The dry periods wrecked the Mycenaean economy and made it tougher to survive.

There are some hints that natural disasters may have hit the region hard, too. Earthquakes and volcanic eruptions disrupted civilization, causing devastation evidenced in the damaged walls of palace complexes. Broken pottery was also found, shattered in a way that points to earth-based disruption (*Decline of the Mycenaean Civilization (1250-1050 B.C.E.)*, 2022).

Finally, human patterns of migration, or invasion, may have unsettled the previously wealthy, advanced Mycenaeans. With population declines and the shifting of resources to basic survival, the Mycenaeans would have been swamped by incoming "Dorian" migrants, or the more war-like Sea Peoples who appeared during the same time period.

These two groups were less technologically and culturally advanced. Called the Dorian Invasion, this mass migration appears to have impacted the native Mycenaean culture, demolished the palace complex system, and led to a decline in cultural activity.

Theories About the Dorian Invasion

The word invasion brings to mind war. You might be envisioning armies charging down hills, pitched battles on the slopes of Greece's mountains, or perhaps long, punishing sieges. The Dorian Invasion, however, is a bit of a misnomer since there is no evidence of large-scale military involvement. The "invasion" would be more aptly named "migration," since the people who moved in with the Mycenaeans were not further advanced in military matters. The Mycenaeans were not conquered.

Historical accounts of this time by ancient historians are now considered to be unreliable at best. After all, knowledge of this period was passed down orally and may have suffered from errors accrued over time. Imagine a telephone game lasting centuries. Facts are certain to have been lost along the way.

Therefore, when Herodotus recounts "The Return of the Heracleidae," or the "Return of Hercules," many scholars suggest taking his story with a grain of salt. Hercules? Isn't he a myth? Indeed, many of the people involved in the story are considered mythical in nature or only barely representative of real people.

In Herodotus's story, Hercules's descendants decided to take back the Peloponnesian peninsula and reclaim Greece for their own. Their efforts were not initially rewarded with success. Several battles resulted in failure, and lives were lost. However, when they teamed up with the Dorians, the descendants of Hercules were able to take over the entire peninsula, thus plunging the original inhabitants into a dark age.

By all accounts, and from the evidence of ruins and artifacts dated to this period, no such invasion took place. It is clear, though, that the Dorians did come from the north, possibly Macedonia or Thessaly. This part of the world was a large region. Today, it would cover the eastern edge of Albania, northern Greece, eastern Bulgaria, North Macedonia, and the southern portion of Kosovo. Still, even if a large portion of migrants appeared on the doorstep of Greece, the robust Mycenaeans should have handled it easily enough. Perhaps something even more devastating had happened—revolution.

Evidence of fires in the great palaces points to some kind of social upheaval. Some scholars believe that constant attacks from the Sea People, a piratical group, might have destabilized the region. Others suggest that in-fighting among the Mycenaean leaders may have torn the war-like civilization apart. Another theory still posits that an uprising of a slave class, which could have included Dorians, brought the social system down. Any of these theories explain why the upper class, including the elite warriors, disappeared so quickly, and why the entire peninsula was overrun with northern tribes (*Dorian Invasion*, 2023).

To this day, there has been no single satisfactory answer, leading many to believe that there may have been a confluence of events that triggered Mycenae's collapse. Regardless of how it happened, it is evident that the decline of the Mycenaeans and an increase of Doric culture signaled a rapid shift. Overnight, in archaeological terms, the world of ancient Greece had changed.

Life in the Dark Ages

Silence. Uncertainty. Struggle. Chaos. These are four words that many might attach to the Greek Dark Ages.

After millennia of keeping records and other writing, creative work, and trade, the post-Mycenaean landscape looks eerily silent in comparison. Archaeological digs have revealed the abandonment of city centers, pointing to an era of uncertainty and struggle. But was the Dorian Invasion as chaotic as some historians have made it out to be?

Social Structures Reorganized

With the Dorian Invasion, society was turned upside down. The *wanax* and the *heqetai* disappeared, leaving a power vacuum for any who might wish to seize control. Depending on the region, the migrating Doric culture either integrated with the native Mycenaeans or overruled them.

Corinth, Argos, and Rhodes saw the two merging cultures blend together relatively well. On the other hand, evidence in Crete and Sparta suggests that the incoming northern tribes ruled the native population through a militarized political system (Varsity Tutor, n.d.).

In other places, political organization crumbled even further with a return to tribal factions and large family clans. These kinship groups or households, known as *oikoi*, split up the regions and fragmented the more cohesive units that the Mycenaeans had built. In Nichoria, for example, archaeologists discovered that a previous Mycenaean town had been abandoned and then rebuilt as a smaller village a century later. Some artifacts at Nichoria suggested that the village had been led by a chieftain, but there was no significant gap in wealth between the leader and his village (McLean, n.d.).

Literacy and Arts Transformed

The state of visual and literary art throughout Greece's Dark Age provides a complex picture of loss and recovery. Since the previous rulers and elite were removed, access to the literacy of Mycenaean culture was lost. The spoken and written language of Linear B faded, replaced by Doric Greek.

This new dialect eventually adopted a new writing system. By the 700s B.C.E., the Phoenician alphabet was most widely used. It wasn't based on pictures, like pictograms, or syllables, like logograms, but instead introduced the idea of having a character for specific sounds. This was the Greeks' first alphabetic writing system (McLean, n.d.).

This change did not happen overnight. As a result, for a long period of time, no accounts were written, and literacy languished. Similarly, the arts also struggled at first as the two cultures figured out how to recover the lost advancements of the late Bronze Age.

That said, the Dorians had forms of art and architecture, as well. Dorian styles of poetry would impact forms of Greek tragedy. It was during this period that Homer wrote his famous epics. In 776 B.C.E., the Olympics were also held for the first time (*History of Greece: The Dark Ages*, 2023).

Dorian ideals of art were linked to simplicity, restraint, and large proportions that would later influence Roman architecture. Compared to the *megarons* and *tholoi* of the Mycenaeans, these new buildings might have seemed rudimentary, but the Dorian people's architecture spoke to a rebirth of creative vision.

Economy Redefined

Another common belief about the Dark Ages was that everyone became a bit poorer. This is true for the most part, as the social hierarchies crumbled and the necessary infrastructure to maintain trade also died. In the beginning, the remaining populations as well as the new migrants were more likely to focus on farming and raising livestock as a means to survive (Greek Boston, 2017b).

At first, these newly created communities couldn't trade or conquer other areas around the Aegean Sea. However, over time, the Dorian civilization began to reach across the ocean. They not only settled in the Cycladic Isles but also sailed further to Rhodes and Crete.

By the 700s B.C.E., trade was once again beginning to flourish. Archeological sites dated to the same period have revealed that the Levant, in particular, began to reestablish trade with the ancient Greeks. With the rise in economic stability, other cultural activities like making art, decorating homes, and investing in nicer burial sites also restarted (McLean, n.d.).

Athens Reborn

Compared to the breadth of the Minoan and later the Mycenaean civilization, the Dorian Invasion period was characterized by a lower population density. As noted before, this might have been due to natural disasters, civil war, or difficulties with farming during arid seasons. What is interesting is that major settlements appear to have been abandoned wholesale at first (Greek Boston, 2017b).

Not only were the palaces and military fortifications abandoned, but many of the major settlements fell into disrepair, some into complete abandonment. When archaeologists looked at the various ancient sites across the Peloponnese, they noted that 90% of the sites had been abandoned. This suggests that the population must have declined sharply (McLean, n.d.).

However, as time went on, the area began to fill once again. Some cities, like Athens, remained dominant. Athens, like a few others, managed to keep a certain level of wealth, and life went on as usual. Its rise to power would set the stage for a new world order.

A New World Order on the Horizon

While the Mycenaean civilization might be praised as being entrepreneurial and cultivated, there was an aspect of their society that was immensely rigid. The class system resulted in a serious divide between those who had power, those who had land, and those who had neither. That all changed during the Dorian Invasion.

With the disappearance of the elite leaders and warriors of Mycenae, a more loose-knit formation emerged within the new communities. Once again divided by geography, these isolated settlements would form what would become known as the *polis*, or Greek city-state.

However, unlike the fortress settlements of Mycenae, the residents were much more independent,
and the social stratification of the previous millennium relaxed slightly. Hereditary rule was forgotten,
and new forms of government emerged, paving the
way for Greece's first form of democracy (*History of
Greece: The Dark Ages*, 2023).

The Origins of Homer

Although the people of Greece's Dark Ages were
not writing books or making records, like all humans,
they loved a good story. The practice of passing stories down by word of mouth was common during this
time as the Dorians and Mycenaeans shared their tales of the past. Through the centuries, some of the
best stories evolved into long tales of heroic warriors
and the gods, perhaps recalling historical events of
the earlier Mycenaean and Minoan civilizations.

Homer's Tales

As noted in the previous chapter, the tales of
Homer were an attempt at inscribing oral traditions
of mythical-historical accounts. Modern-day scholars
initially believed it was no more than a myth because
of the references to the Greek pantheon. The dates
linked to Homer also suggested that the time period
between Homer (8th century B.C.E.) and the actual
events he recounted was over 400 years. Homer's two
famous poems, the *Iliad* and *Odyssey* would inspire

the ancient Greeks and form part of the backbone of Western literature. But their origin is problematic.

In the *Iliad*, Homer describes the war between the armies of King Agamemnon of Mycenae and King Priam of Troy. The source of the conflict was Menelaus's beautiful wife, Helen. According to the English playwright Christopher Marlowe, Helen was so beautiful, she had a "face that launched a thousand ships" (Marlowe, 1604).

When she left Menelaus to be with Paris of Troy, the king of Sparta and his brother Agamemnon decided to get her back. They gathered armies, and with a cohort of warriors, such as Achilles and Odysseus, they laid siege to Troy for 10 years. Many died on both sides, but eventually, relying on the cunning of Odysseus, the Greeks were able to deceive the Trojans, enter the city hidden in a wooden horse, and sack Troy.

In Homer's *Iliad*, the poet describes the first part of the war, the death of Paris's brother Hector at the hands of Achilles, and the treaty that brings the siege to a short pause. Virgil's work *Aeneid* describes in detail how the Greeks deceived Troy and the aftermath. Virgil's poem describes more of the connection between the Romans and Greek history, probably as a way to affirm the political and cultural legitimacy of Rome.

The other major poem Homer wrote, the *Odyssey*, focuses on Odysseus' return home. During this saga, Odysseus endures a long, winding journey home to Ithaca. It is filled with adventures and obstacles, which he has to overcome with his wisdom, experience, and cunning.

When he finally reaches home, he discovers that his wife is being courted by other men because she is considered a widow. However, his faithful wife and son, Penelope and Telemachus, are waiting for him. Together, father and son unite to kill the suitors and reestablish Odysseus as King of Ithaca (The Editors of Encyclopedia Britannica, 2019).

Oral Traditions

While we might find the stories of the *Iliad* and *Odyssey* exciting and inspiring, they are, unfortunately, not the complete picture. They are all that remains of a larger body of work that has been lost to time.

Most scholars believe that many stories were spoken and not written down during the earlier centuries of the Dark Ages. Passed down by word of mouth, the poems were probably memorized and shared by professional bards called *rhapsodes* who would stitch together stories from memorized poetic formulae. They may have been used as entertainment during religious festivals. In later periods, at school, they were some of the first stories read by students (Homer's World, 2011).

In many ways, the oral traditions (and then, later, Homer's poems) were similar to what we call historical fiction or historical epics. Like the "historical fiction" films *Braveheart* and *Gladiator*, these orally transmitted stories took the seeds of what might have been historical events and added a load of exciting drama and adventure that says as much about the culture producing the new versions as the original events the stories portray, perhaps more. Initially, this caused confusion among modern scholars, who saw the tales as simply made up.

However, with the discovery of the actual site of Troy, it became clear that oral poetry played an important role in culture-making during and after the Dorian Invasion. The poems highlight the sense of nostalgia that arose during the Dark Ages when Greeks looked back at a golden era for inspiration. These stories more than likely helped to unify the groups who settled in the area and to validate political ambitions as the city-states, the *poleis*, emerged at the end of the Dark Ages. Even more importantly, the passing down of oral tales allowed future Greeks to preserve the stories of the Dark Ages. During the Archaic Period, Homer's transcription of the poetry would play an important role in culture-making once again.

The Emergence of the Polis

In the last century of the Dark Ages, between 850–750 B.C.E., the previously loose-knit communities, isolated by mountains and sea, began to stabilize politically once again. However, instead of returning to the rigid hierarchies of the *wanax*, the *heqetai*, and the other ancient strata, the new communities, now formed of Dorian migrants and Mycenaean natives, began to organize themselves into new forms of governance.

As before, the villages and cities struggled to form a single nation. The mountains and the Aegean Sea proved to be obstacles yet again for unity, particularly after the breakdown of the Mycenaean social order. The emergence of the *polis*, the city-state, formalized as one of the most important political frameworks in ancient Greece, each with its own unique cultural and political landscape.

While some city-states were ruled by monarchs, others were ruled by groups of select people, forming what is called an oligarchy. Less fortunate cities were seized by tyrants. Tyrannies generally did not end well, but for some of these cities, they were a welcome change from the anarchy and chaos of the previous centuries. Indeed, some poleis installed their tyrants by popular acclamation. The popular tyrants, in turn, often provided housing and jobs.

However, after years of upheaval, a new form of government took the stage—the first form of democracy. The democracy of these new city-states wasn't the same as the voting rights and processes that we enjoy today. However, the small advances leading out of the Greek Dark Ages signaled a step forward into a brand-new form of government that would change history and transform the world.

Darkness Before the Dawn

For a long time, scholars depicted Greece's Dark Age as a time when poverty ruled, literacy disappeared, and culture struggled to survive. While it is true that the Mycenaeans faced a time of economic and cultural struggle, new research and investigations reveal that the Dorian Invasion did not spell an absolute end.

Instead, the Dark Ages repositioned Greece economically, socially, and politically. As the Dark Ages lifted, a new dawn approached for Greece. The forthcoming era, known as the Archaic Period, ushered in unparalleled innovations in art, politics, and society. Join us in the next chapter as we explore the foundations of the classical civilization that would inspire the world.

Part 2: The Rise of the *Polis*

and Classical Greece

Chapter 4: The Archaic Period

A wide grey road wound its way through the rolling green hills of Greece's countryside, past rustic farmhouses huddled in villages, and toward the walled fortification of an early city. Then, it arrived at the heart of every Greek *polis*—the *agora*.

The large square was filled with wooden stalls where the citizens of the *polis* gathered every day to do business. Here, they bought the latest catch of fish, bartered for cloth, pottery, and farm produce, and caught up on the latest gossip. Around the agora, other citizens involved in the governance of the city met—in the law courts, where disputes were settled; the stoa, where the citizens of the *polis* gathered to talk; the *bouleuterion*, where the city council met; and the *prytanikon*, where members of the council lived.

This was the heart of the *polis*, but also the heart of Greece. What fueled the emergence and expansion of the Greek city-states? By answering this question, we will understand how the many *poleis* transformed Greece and thus, the world.

The Foundation and General Characteristics of the Poleis

From about 800–480 B.C.E., Greek culture and society emerged from the shadows of the Dark Age into what scholars call the Archaic Period. Human records and cultural activity began to proliferate once again as the populations coalesced back into larger settlements. The mountainous landscape ensured that these new cities would remain isolated, and ambitious aristocrats and kings were less likely to give up authority over their growing city-states.

Of the 1,000 *poleis* that sprang up, Athens, Delphi, Corinth, Thebes, Rhodes, Syracuse, and Sparta were arguably the most famous influential. Athens and Sparta were the most powerful and held the most territory (The Greek Polis, 2017).

The political and cultural landscape of each *polis* varied, but there were some commonalities. Politically, four major political systems evolved as the city-states proliferated across Greece and the Aegean Sea: monarchies, oligarchies, tyrannies, and democracies (Greek City-States, 2022).

In terms of city planning, most poleis shared common features, including:

- **chora** - which are the surrounding farms and villages.

- **fortification walls** – Sparta was the most notable exception.

- **urban centers** - with gymnasiums, temples, amphitheaters, an agora, and (geography permitting) an acropolis.

The agora, in particular, was a square area in the center of the city where trade and governance were carried out. Public and government buildings surrounded it. On the other hand, temples and theaters were often placed further away, such as on the hills. This was because the locations chosen were either sacred or because they simply looked more aesthetically pleasing in a natural setting.

Most *poleis* were also invested in creating singular identities that all of its inhabitants could be proud of and connected to. Their focus on the agora, *polis-*

specific festivals, mythical founders, and patron deities helped to form unique societies for each *polis*. This way, citizens (land-owning males) and non-citizens (everyone else) could feel united under a single banner, regardless of their representation or lack thereof (Cartwright, 2013).

Overall, *poleis* represented groups of people who had gathered for mutual economic and political benefits. Their goods, products, coinage, art, and political organization often varied. Of all of the city-states, three make representative case studies: Corinth, Athens, and Sparta.

Corinth

Strictly transliterated as *Korinthos*, Corinth was an ancient city located at the most important intersection of Greece—the Isthmus of Corinth. The large peninsula of Greece is actually comprised of two parts connected by a thin strand of land, also known as an isthmus. The two-sided harbor city, therefore, fronted the two most important seas in the Greek World—the Ionian Sea to the west and the Aegean Sea to the east (Ancient Corinth, 2023).

As noted earlier, Corinth, like most *poleis*, was filled with government buildings, temples, and other public spaces, like the agora. An important location in Corinth was the Fountain of Peirene, which was considered sacred and was therefore developed over time to become more like a temple (Ancient Corinth, 2023). Other temples honored Apollo, Poseidon, and cult heroes like King Sisyphus, Bellerophon, Jason, and Medea.

Its major features, however, were its two harbors: Lechaion, on the Corinthian Gulf to the west, and Kenchreai on the Saronic Gulf to the east. Between the two harbors, a special stone track was created, called the Diolkos. It allowed the Corinthians to drag large wagonloads of produce—or even ships—from one harbor to the other (Cartwright, 2009). This innovative way of portage allowed traders to avoid sailing around the southern peninsula.

Because of this, Corinth flourished as a trade city. It relied on maritime trade to sell the goods it became known for—glass jars, perfumes, pottery, wine bronze, and furs. Corinthians were able to trade with other parts of Greece and Italy, as well as with the Phoenicians. Their perfume pots became particularly famous when they invented a new form of artistic black-figure pottery (Carr, 2017). They dominated the pottery market for a couple of centuries, boosting their wealth and allowing for a more stabilized society.

Corinth had a dynamic political history. Emerging from a strict monarchical system, Corinth shifted into a time of flux, where it was either run by oligarchs or tyrants. The Cypselid tyrants made a name for themselves, particularly the second tyrant, Periander, who came to power in the early 600s B.C.E.

According to Herodotus, Periander was initially more interested in encouraging the arts and ruled his people reasonably. However, after taking advice from

Thrasybulus, another tyrant running the city-state Miletus, Periander began to believe that the only way to consolidate power was to weed out the powerful and rich Corinthian citizens. Periander became increasingly blood-thirsty and suspicious. He killed his wife, ostracized his favored son, and terrorized the citizens of Corinth until his death (Lloyd, 2016). Eventually, Corinth would transform into an oligarchic state with limited democratic elements, including a council of 80 elders. This ensured citizens had some input in the governance of their city (Cartwright, 2018a).

Around the same time, Corinth began to expand culturally. Corinth became famous for the Isthmian Games, which were similar to the Olympic Games. In honor of Poseidon, they were held at Isthmia every two years during the spring. Its horse and chariot races were particularly famous (Cartwright, 2009).

Corinth would never gain the power that Athens and Sparta had, but it is a good example of how ancient Greek politics transformed over time from the Dark Ages onward. It exemplifies the struggles for political freedom, economic independence, and innovation, as well as cultural production. Unlike intellectual Athens or war-like Sparta, Corinth struggled to establish a stable government. In the end, it became a major player in the late 5th-century war between Athens and Sparta (see Chapter 5).

Athens

Athens, also known as *Athenai*, is the most famous city-state of Ancient Greece, founded in the region of Attica. It made its mark on history with its art, culture, and politics. For its time, Athens was an impressive sight to behold. It was a beautiful city, set on a plain surrounded by hills and the Aegean.

Athens had everything most city-states had: a hilltop fort on an acropolis, temples, sacred shrines, monuments, and government buildings. Although it was surrounded by hills, the countryside did not yield enough produce for the city; the climate of Attica was drier than the more fertile regions of Sparta.

Athens, therefore, relied heavily on its harbor to increase its economic and political power throughout the Archaic period. It developed silver mines to increase the value of its products, relied on alliances with other *poleis* for trade, and gained dominance over many of the Cycladic Islands (Williams, 2008).

Internally, Athens struggled at first. Its political scene, tending toward an oligarchical structure, led to corruption, oppression, and a widening class gap. Many lower-class citizens ended up impoverished to the point they would sell themselves into debt slavery.

This led to revolt and systemic changes, led by Draco, an Athenian statesman, who first revised Athenian law. His first statutes, created around 620 B.C.E., were too harsh. Many crimes were punishable by death, leading to the creation of the word "draco-nian," which means "overly severe" (The Greek Polis, 2017).

Soon after, Solon stepped in to revise Draco's laws. He tried to equalize the political structure and allow the common classes to have a voice. Not only did Solon ease Draco's harsh laws but he also can-celed debts, abolished debt slavery, and laid the groundwork for democracy in Athens. The common people were allowed to take part in the government and be heard. Solon divided male Athenians into four classes based on wealth and defining their military responsibility:

- *pentakosiomedimnoi* - the "five-hundred-bushel men" (highest)

- *hippeis* – knights, or the cavalry class

- *zeugitai* - the hoplite class

- *thetes* - the rowing class (lowest)

The state was therefore hierarchical, but no longer based on birth alone. Now, it also took into consideration land-owning or military capabilities (Hornblower, 2023).

The restrictive hierarchy Solon had instituted colored its attempts at democracy. The only citizens who could vote were males who owned land. That meant that of its 300,000 citizens, only 20% were actually eligible to vote (Williams, 2008). Women, foreigners, slaves, and anyone who didn't own land couldn't vote. While debt slavery was abolished, Athens relied on its slave class to cultivate food in the surrounding countryside, do construction work, mine, quarry, and carry out domestic duties (The Greek Polis, 2017).

Women, regardless of their station, did not have many freedoms. They were expected to remain home to tend to their family's households. If they wished to go out or travel, they required a male chaperone. Unlike boys, Athenian girls were not sent to school and faced a life of relative security, depending on their class, but also many restrictions (Athens vs. Sparta - Difference and Comparison, 2019).

Athens wasn't paradise, but after the Dorian Invasion and the Dark Ages, it was considered the height of culture for its time. More educated and intellectual, the city focused on learning, strategy, and cerebral or artistic pursuits. Boys studied history, literature, philosophy, math, science, rhetoric, military strategy, and art, among other things.

As its navy grew in power and its territory increased, Athens became more wealthy and secure, allowing its citizens to foster the arts and pursue academics (Noonan, 2023). Although an outlier in its size and influence, Athens' steps toward democracy are representative of a wider trend in many other Greek *poleis*.

Sparta

If any *polis* offers a sharp contrast to Athens, it's Sparta (also known as *Lakedaimon*). Located in Laconia, a fertile area in the southern Peloponnesian peninsula, Sparta was nestled among fertile hills, perfect for growing crops and raising livestock. Up through the 600s B.C.E., the city, its population, and its territory slowly grew to encompass the whole of Laconia (The Greek Polis, 2017).

However, despite its massive size, Sparta did not gain a huge population. This might have been because Sparta was isolated. And, since it was self-sustainable, it did not contact other city-states or encourage immigration.

Sparta was naturally defended. The city did not require the walled fortifications that Athens and other *poleis* had. Instead, the city clustered about the usual buildings—the agora, the acropolis, the temples, and government buildings.

When excavations of the Archaic period layers were dug up, archaeologists discovered that there weren't as many temples, monuments, and statues as in other *poleis*. This was because Sparta was not as focused on art and intellectual pursuits. As a result, Sparta's pottery tended to be minimalist, geometric, and utilitarian, but with its own beauty. Skilled workers in Sparta created vase paintings, bone or ivory carvings, stone sculptures, and metalwork.

Sparta was more interested in athletics and military prowess. Its entire political structure became centered around its citizens' ability to participate in war. The hierarchical structure of Sparta, however, was rather complex, involving a monarchy and a mild blend of oligarchy and representative council. This hierarchy included:

- **two kings** from two powerful families

- **the gerousia**, a council of elders

- **the ephors**, five representatives chosen by lot from the citizen body

- **the hoplites**, the population of full-citizen males

- **the helots**, the unfree laborers working in the farmland outside the city

The hoplites were very important. Taken at the age of seven, these boys were raised in barracks, away from their families, where they were trained for war. In their early teens, they would take part in the fighting.

While these males had some rights, inevitably, wealthy families would enjoy more privileges than others. Below, the helots were tied to the land and forced to farm for Sparta while secured by Sparta's warriors.

Since physical strength, size, and military prowess were prized above all else, if you were more intellectually inclined or physically weak, you would struggle to maintain any meaningful status within the city. Sparta became known for being harsh, and their ruthless habit of killing weak or small infants has shocked historians throughout the centuries.

However, although Spartan culture was cruel, it was a culture of paradoxes. The kings, with their oligarchies, listened to the ephors. Similarly, while strong males were preferred, women were given more freedom than in other Greek city-states.

Spartan women could not only own property but were also able to control their own finances when widowed. Dowries were given to women, which they often used to buy land. As a result, half of the Spartan land was owned by women.

Furthermore, women were educated, allowed to take part in athletics, drink wine, travel without a male chaperone, and wear what they wanted (The Greek Polis, 2017). With Sparta, we can see yet again how diverse the city-states of ancient Greece were in terms of their ideas of how to order a society.

Colonization and Expansion

During the Archaic Period, city-states with larger populations or less agricultural land, most notably Corinth, began to look for land elsewhere. They would set up trade centers and free markets, called *emporia*, across islands and other abandoned shoreline locations. This was not a concerted effort to create an empire. Rather it originated from a need for more resources and land for their growing populations. As a result, colonization began slowly at the beginning of the 8th century and gained momentum as the mainland Greek poleis became more affluent.

During the colonization period, Greek settlers also began to extend to southern Italy, calling it *"Megale Hellas,"* or "Greater Greece" (*Magna Graecia* in Latin). These colonies were often military in nature, sometimes conquering the locals and impressing their own culture on the populace.

The process of Hellenization, "spreading Greek culture," began. Many of these colonies were sent by Chalcis, Achaea, Phocaea, Athens, and Sparta. Parts of Sicily were also conquered by Rhodes, Crete, and Corinth, among others (Cartwright, 2018c).

Eventually, the Greeks would spread across the rest of the Mediterranean coastline, settling along the shorelines of modern-day France, Spain, Northern Africa, Turkey, and around the Black Sea. All of these colonies, far away from their mother cities (*metropoleis*), carried on their own systems of culture and government. They were not ruled like their parent government necessarily, but many followed the same forms as mentioned before—monarchies, oligarchies, and tyrannies. From these unique city-states, various new forms of artistry emerged, as well as new resources. For example, in the Black Sea region, gold became an important raw commodity (Hemingway, 2019).

Greece was not an empire, but its *poleis*, out of economic necessity, began to populate the known world, trading and competing with the Phoenicians, the Egyptians, and many Middle Eastern peoples. With each trade contact or conquest, their power grew, building the largest city-states into vessels of power that would one day set the stage for a war that would transform Greece.

The Development of Greek Literature

The Dark Ages represented a loss of literacy. But, emerging from that time, a new script was accepted and evolved to fit the scholars and record-keepers of

Archaic Greece. No longer connected to the Mycenaean Linear B script, this new alphabet was formed from the Phoenician writing system, which itself originated in the Middle East. It was related to the Semitic writing systems like ancient Hebrew. According to Herodotus, Phoenicians introduced the alphabet to Ionian Greeks, the Greek colonists located in Western Asia Minor. From there, it quickly spread to the other *poleis* throughout the Greek world.

Unlike the pictograms and logograms of earlier ancient writing systems, the Phoenician alphabet was phonetic and allowed for greater variation in terms of connecting the spoken word to writing. Initially, the Phoenician alphabet was a utilitarian script, consisting of 22 characters with vowel sounds built into the characters. The Greeks added more symbols to represent vowels and evolved the alphabet to fit their language's phonics.

Since the language and the writing system were more flexible, scholarly writing improved and increased. Greeks began to write about everything—science, math, history, literature, and more. They leveraged the versatility of the Phoenician alphabet to collate information on a large scale. This new alphabet later evolved into Classical Greek, and it later impacted the Latin and English alphabets (Mark, 2015b).

After long centuries plunged into silence, the Greek literary world came alive. Its records, plays, poems, and treatises point to a lively culture. Debate was encouraged, and progress was driven by economic, political, and academic interests.

Many of the ideas the Greeks shared had been developed by earlier minds, but their brilliant synthesis was able to push the boundaries of human knowledge. Even so, there still remain many gaps, particularly in the early part of the Archaic period. Many questions remain, such as the mystery of Homer.

The Rise of Homer

Who was Homer? No one really knows. He is a bit of a mysterious figure. No scholar or archaeologist has managed to uncover where he was born, who he was, or when or where he lived. However, ancient Greek and Roman scholars have suggested that he lived in Greece between 900 and 700 B.C.E.

The island of Chios has been linked to Homer as a place where he might have lived, but there are no definitive clues that he resided there. Another characteristic linked to Homer by ancient scholars is that he was blind. Once again, no data has been able to prove this definitively.

Modern historians have floated another popular theory: Homer was not one singular person. It is very possible that the two poems might have been written by more than one person. Bards would often sing together, making up verses as they went. It is, therefore, probable that the epic poems the *Iliad* and the *Odyssey* were the result of a collaborative effort by talented musicians and poets (Homer's World, 2011). Homer could be just a singular name for a group of people who preserved the dying oral traditions of their ancestors.

Preserving the Homeric Tradition

Greece's epic poems had a long history forged from the oral traditions of the Dark Ages. Thankfully, they were eventually written down and formalized by "Homer" during the Archaic period. Utilizing the newly found Greek alphabet, the Greeks were able to preserve and standardize their oral narratives.

However, since they lived during the end of the Dark Ages and the emergence of the Archaic period, this composite "Homer" undoubtedly put his own spin on the tales. It is possible that his version of the poems differs from the original oral traditions that emerged 400 years earlier, after the Dorian Invasion.

Preserving Homer's version of the oral traditions required the work of many individuals throughout history. As with almost all ancient literary works, there is no original manuscript. But thankfully, others copied the original written poems. Eventually, the poems reached their more or less canonical form in the early 2nd century B.C.E., when Aristarchus edited them and placed them in the famous library at Alexandria.

Even then, the texts were in danger of disappearing. Copies were made once again, and the two poems were shared before the tragic fire that destroyed the

Library of Alexandria. The modern versions of Homer's poems, therefore, are the result of careful preservation that may have also altered the details of the stories in the intervening years (Nagy, 2017).

Not a lot may be known about Homer, but it is clear to see that Homer's work, although initially oral, marked the beginning of a cultural recovery. This transformation would take place over the next couple of centuries. By using the new Greek alphabet, he was able to preserve poetry and helped to found renewed literary endeavors. Thanks to Homer's work, not only was a veil drawn back on ancient Greek history, which prompted the search for the city of Troy, but his epic poems also inspired literature, music, and art around the world for millennia (Whelan, 2020).

Setting the Stage

What must this new world have felt like? We can sum it up with two words: the Olympics. Starting in 776 B.C.E., the Olympic Games united the city-states for a short period of time every four years. It provided cities with a chance to show off their athleticism, show civic pride, and honor their patron deity. Winners were gifted with laurels, and the audience enjoyed a rare unity with other *poleis* (International Olympic Committee, 2021).

In many ways, the origins of the Olympic Games highlight the vigor of discovery and growth felt during this period. With the increase of resources and territories, the Greek *poleis* flourished, spread their ideas, and left their imprint on the ancient world. This was a precursor to what would be known as the Hellenic identity.

Another thing that would unite the city-states during this time of prosperity was the threat of war. Set against the Persian Empire, the *poleis* arranged themselves into loosely knit alliances. The epic confrontations between the Greeks and Persians would forever alter history. Join us in Chapter 5 as we explore the tumultuous era of Classical Greece and witness the splendor of Greek civilization at its zenith.

Chapter 5: Classical Greece

Steep mountainsides cascaded down on either side. Ahead of them, a road led north, now filled with rank upon rank of spears and horses. The forces of the Persian King had arrived. All that stood between them and their goal were several thousand men huddled behind the barely repaired ruins of a wall. It was going to be a piece of cake, they must have thought. A single push, and they'd be through. They were wrong.

From 480 to 350 B.C.E., Greece flourished in more ways than one. Not only was it able to prove to the world at large that it was a military force to be reckoned with, but it also witnessed the growth of sophisticated culture hitherto unseen in these regions of the world. Classical Greece was a time of unparalleled glory and bitter conflict, when mighty heroes and city-states shaped the destiny of Western civilization.

However, the golden age was brought to an end by the greed and ambition of two city-states—Athens and Sparta. Who would be the winner? Or would the so-called victor realize that, in winning, they too had lost?

The Greco-Persian Wars

The Greek *poleis* were flourishing. A period of expansion across the Mediterranean Sea had led to wealth for their citizens and a growing sense of pride in themselves. Greece was not alone, though. There were other nations, like the Persian Empire, who also had dreams of expansion and an equal drive for resources. It was only a matter of time until they would clash.

The origins of the Greco-Persian Wars began when the Persian Empire expanded into Asia Minor (modern Turkey) in the mid-6th century B.C.E. Ionian Greeks had settled there in the age of colonization, creating or immigrating to major port cities like Byzantium, Ephesus, and Sinope. Some of these cities, largely non-Greek, accepted Persian rule and became part of its western provinces, also known as satrapies.

Some colonies with strong ties to their *metropoleis* attempted unsuccessfully to revolt between 499 and 493 B.C.E. (Gill, 2019). The Athenians helped rebel forces besiege the provincial capital of

Sardis in 498 B.C.E., torching much of the city. They were ultimately unsuccessful. The revolting colonies were brought in line. King Darius I of Persia, however, wasn't going to forget the interfering role of Athens and her allies (Bliss, 2022).

Two Invasions

The Persian Wars are divided into two major invasions followed by counterattacks. Separated by years of fighting, the invasions pitted Persia against many prominent Greek city-states. Persia, however, invaded the mainland of Greece before being pushed back once and for all.

In order to fend off the Persians, the Greeks uneasily allied with each other. Athens led a new league, the Delian League, which it formed in 479 B.C.E. Most of the city-states joined the Delian League, but Sparta remained independent.

Each *polis* had a single vote in the League, but Athens was the leader. While they battled the Persians together, the Delian League *poleis* and Sparta were also trying to outdo one another. But who would win?

The Battles and Warriors of the Persian Wars

While Persian invasions and the resulting counterattacks involved many battles, four stood out to ancient historians for their cultural and historical significance: the battles of Marathon, Thermopylae, Salamis, and Plataea. These battles were significant in deciding who ultimately won the war. They also highlighted the strength of combined Greek military power, setting the stage for later conquests.

The Battle of Marathon

In 490 B.C.E., the Battle of Marathon was held on a plain outside the city of Marathon. Facing King Darius I's forces (anywhere between 25,000 and 90,000 men), the Greeks proved they could withstand the power of the superior forces of the Persians. Led by an Athenian leader, Miltiades, Greek forces numbered only 10,000.

When the Persian fleet landed on the shores of Marathon, they discovered that the Greeks were waiting for them on the narrow plain just beyond. Miltiades thinned the center of his battle line. In this way, as the Persians pushed through, the more densely manned sides of the Greek wings then enveloped the Persian forces. The plain of Marathon was too narrow for the Persian cavalry to counter the maneuver effectively.

Recognizing defeat, the Persians fought their way back to their ships. The battle was brutal. On the shores of Marathon, Miltiades was slain. Most of the Persian fleet escaped; but the Greeks had won (Cartwright, 2013d).

The Battle of Thermopylae

Darius died in 486 B.C.E., and his son Xerxes I prepared a second invasion of Greece. His target was Athens, and the only viable land route was through Thermopylae, a narrow path with a steep mountain on one side and sea cliffs on the other.

In 480 B.C.E., the Greeks sent a mixed group of Spartans, Corinthians, Thebans, Arcadians, and others to create an army of around 7,000 men. They faced off against a Persian force of 80,000 troops. King Xerxes waited four days for the army to flee. They refused to budge. He ordered them to drop their weapons. King Leonidas of Sparta sent back a suitably laconic reply: *Molōn labe*—come and get them.

The Persians did. Leonidas and the Greek forces held out for three days. However, their time was cut short by a traitorous shepherd who gave intel to the Persian army. Using a hidden path, the Persians looped around and attacked from the south, surrounding King Leonidas and his surviving fighters.

With no one to stop them, the Persians sacked Athens and took a strip of territory on the mainland. Nevertheless, the Greeks were already preparing new forces to halt the Persian invasion. In later years, despite the fact that the Greeks had lost, the Battle of Thermopylae became a popular tale of a band of men fighting for freedom against all odds (Cartwright, 2013a).

The Battle of Salamis

Soon after the loss at Thermopylae, in September of 480 B.C.E., the Greeks were forced yet again to face King Xerxes and his army; this time, at sea. The Battle of Salamis, a naval battle between the Greeks and Persians, was Greece's last chance to stop Persia from taking over the mainland. The Greeks, comprising about 300 ships led by Themistocles, an Athenian general with previous victories under his belt, faced a huge Persian navy of almost 1,200 ships, made up of fleets from Egypt, Phoenicia, Persia proper, and even some Ionian Greek cities.

When the navies drew close, the Greeks deployed, probably in two ranks, with their backs to the island of Salamis. The cramped Saronic Gulf meant that the Persians could not bring their entire fleet to bear at once. The Greek navy drew the Persians into the strait and the ships began maneuvering to ram each other. It is difficult to reconstruct the tactical dispositions of the opposing sides, but the Persian sailors were more experienced, and the ancient sources affirm the Greek ships were heavier and slower than the invaders.

Nevertheless, the Greek navy controlled the battlefield of the waves. Their ships likely carried contingents of 20 heavily armed hoplite marines each, while the skilled crews of the Persians were less well armed. Moreover, while the Persians had been rowing practically all night, the Greeks were relatively fresh.

As more Persian ships moved forward, they cut off exits from their allies who floundered among the Greek ships. Some of Persia's navy ran aground, others were sunk, and some were able to extract themselves and return home. This allowed the Greeks to move their hoplite army to the mainland, where they began to attack the remaining Persians. King Xerxes was forced to retreat (Cartwright, 2013b).

The Battle of Plataea

From Salamis onward, King Xerxes remained at home, leaving the invasion in the hands of General Mardonius, a gifted Persian leader and cousin to the king. It wasn't until 479 B.C.E., the year after the naval victory at Salamis, that the Greeks were able to force Persia off the mainland once and for all. The Battle of Plataea would be the birthplace of Greece's freedom.

During this battle, the Persians fielded around 130,000 men. Opposing them, the combined forces of Athens, Sparta, and other city-states gathered in the mightiest Greek army yet, comprising around 70,000. The two armies were very different from one another. The Persians preferred to soften up their targets with long-range attacks from archers, which they would then follow up with a devastating cavalry charge. The Greeks preferred to use a tight-knit formation on foot, called a phalanx, that was heavily armored but slower in movement.

The leadup to the battle lasted 11 days. It was a cat-and-mouse game. Both sides tried to lure the other into their preferred location. The Greeks wanted to fight the Persians in the foothills while the Persians wanted to lure the Greeks out onto the plain.

As days passed, dwindling water and food supplies became a problem. Led by Pausanius, a Spartan leader, a major part of the army began to retreat in search of water. When the Persians pursued, they found themselves inadvertently flanked by stranded Athenians and Plataeans when the war-ready Spartans turned at bay. The Greeks were outnumbered, but heavily armed. When Mardonius was killed by a rock thrown by a Spartan, the Persian troops nearby began a retreat that swiftly devolved into a rout. The Greeks were finally able to stem the tide of Persia and prepare for a counterattack (Gill, 2019a).

The Fallout

Greece successfully defended itself from a Persian invasion. It sustained attacks from the massive empire, and from the fires of war, it emerged stronger than ever.

Not only was Greece able to stop the Persians from penetrating into Europe, but it was able to reclaim many of its Ionian settlements along the edges of the Black and Aegean Seas. Recognizing the Greeks' combined strength, Persia opted to encourage the tensions between Sparta and Athens.

The widening split between the two grew in the following years. Differences in culture, leadership, and governance became apparent. Joining forces with powerful city-states like Corinth, Sparta reformed the Peloponnesian League that had been first created around 550 B.C.E. On the other hand, Athens ran the Delian League, which became less of an alliance and more of an Athenian hegemony as it browbeat weaker *poleis* to remain loyal (*Effects of the Persian Wars*, 2023). The question was: Which league would win?

The Golden Age

The Greco-Persian Wars were a dark time for Greece. Many lives were lost. However, an awareness of power emerged within the city-states, particularly in Sparta and Athens. National pride began to grow. As the *poleis* began to rebuild, many of their leaders dreamed of a glorious future for their people, and Athens was at the center of it all.

Pericles: The First Citizen of Athens

After the intense conflict of Greco-Persian Wars, Pericles (495-429 B.C.E.) came to power in Athens. He was a studious introvert who did not seek political power. When he met Aspasia of Miletus, the beautiful and wise woman encouraged him to use his skills for the good of the people.

Pericles' influence grew, and from 461 to 429 B.C.E. he exerted a great deal of control over Athens. He was a talented statesman, orator, and general who oversaw a flourishing of Athenian and, by extension, Greek culture. This period of time is often called the Age of Pericles because his influence changed Athens and the rest of Greece, even beyond his death.

Pericles further developed Greece's early forms of democracy. Male citizens of Athens could vote and participate in politics. He also ensured that Athens remained a powerful city-state among the other *poleis*.

Ever conscious of the destruction the Persians wrought on Athens, Pericles carefully used the Delian League to his home city's advantage. This led, in time, to the Peloponnesian Wars between Athens and Sparta. However, it also ensured that Athens' cultural and political achievements would last.

Under Pericles, Athens became a cultural center. Alongside his consort, Aspasia, he promoted Greek art, music, literature, architecture, philosophy, and other advancements. The world he helped nurture would indeed stand the test of time. When Pericles succumbed to the plague in 429 B.C.E., his loss was felt. Athens struggled to replace their leader (Mark, 2018).

The Great Works

During the Age of Pericles, Athens witnessed the growth of cultural, philosophical, and scientific expression. Continuing the trend of the Archaic Period, Greek literary output intensified through the Classical Period, producing some of the most famous pieces of literature in the Western tradition.

In addition to famous Athenian playwrights like Aristophanes and Sophocles, other Greek academics wrote down their advancements in science, history, and philosophy; and many Athenian literary and artistic works are preserved to this day. Some of the most famous writers, thinkers, and artists of this era include (Mamakouka, 2014):

- **Sophocles** (496-406 B.C.E.), a tragic playwright who wrote *Antigone* and *Oedipus the King*, among others.

- **Phidias** (490-430 B.C.E.) was a sculptor, painter, and architect who sculpted for the Parthenon.

- **Herodotus** (484-425 B.C.E.) was an historian who wrote *The Histories* and who was known as "the father of history."

- **Euripides** (480-406 B.C.E.), a tragic playwright who wrote plays about Medea and Helen

- **Socrates** (c. 470-399 B.C.E.) was a philosopher known as the "father of philosophy."

- **Democritus** (460-370 B.C.E.) was a philosopher who developed the idea of atoms as the building block of the material universe.

- **Hippocrates** (460-370 B.C.E.), a doctor who created the Hippocratic Oath and wrote treatises on medicine and doctoral ethics; also known as the "father of medicine."

- **Aristophanes** (446-386 B.C.E.), a comic playwright who wrote *The Birds, The Frogs,* and *Lysistrata,* among others.

- **Plato** (424-348 B.C.E.), a philosopher who wrote *The Republic* and *Symposium,* and who produced philosophical "dialogues" between Socrates and other Greek thinkers.

The Peloponnesian Wars: Athens vs. Sparta

The Age of Pericles marked the growth of Athens in many ways. Now home to around 300,000 people, Athens was fast becoming an important political center. It was the heart of the Delian League, and the source of great wealth thanks to its navy and trade connections.

Although it had been sacked by the Persians, Athens rebuilt stronger than ever under Pericles. Its alliances with other city-states, though soured by its ambitions, remained mostly secure. There was one polis, however, that sought to eclipse Athens—Sparta (Woerner, 2022).

Roots of Conflict

After the end of the Greco-Persian Wars, the uneasy truce between the Delian League and Sparta came to an end. Scholars suggest that Sparta feared Athens's ambitions and didn't think the Greek *poleis* had the resources to conquer the Persian Empire. In some ways, Sparta was right.

Athens' handling of the Delian League betrayed its intentions. Despite increasing revolts within the

League, Athens began to clash with Sparta. Other factors for the Peloponnesian War stemmed from the stark differences between the two city-states. Sparta was a *polis* that focused on military might, while Athens valued education, art, and trade.

Recognizing that Athens held greater power, Sparta worried that Athens would turn its eyes to the fertile lands that Sparta held. Therefore, in 460 B.C.E., the First Peloponnesian War broke out, plunging all of Greece into armed conflict as the two leagues clashed. Fighting continued off and on for 25 years, until 445 B.C.E. During this period, Athens and Argos clashed with Sparta and Thebes.

Athens ruled the seas due to their experience in naval warfare. Sparta fought hard to maintain dominance on land. In the Battle of Tanagra, Sparta beat Athens. It was a sign of things to come.

There were several attempts at peace. Initially, a treaty was brokered by the moderate Athenian general Cimon in 446 B.C.E. It was supposed to last 30 years. However, disputes over land, such as the sacred site of Delphi, as well as revolts in Athenian-held Megara, led to further degradation of the relationship between Athens and Sparta.

The ultimate spark, however, was Corinth, which had long opposed Athens and considered itself Sparta's ally. When Corinth entered conflict with Athens, Sparta came to its aid, starting a 27-year war that threatened to tear Greek culture down from its lofty height (National Geographic Society, 2022b).

Athens vs. Sparta

In 431 B.C.E., Sparta was back at war with Athens. The Second Peloponnesian War, which lasted from 431 to 404 B.C.E., had begun.

Led by the eloquent and charismatic general Brasidas, Spartan forces clashed with Athenian armies. At first, neither side could gain the upper hand. Athens, struggling with plague in 429 B.C.E., lost its brilliant leader Pericles. Still, it pushed its forces into the Corinthian Gulf and attacked Sparta's allies. At the same time, Sparta began a two-year siege of Plataea, which eventually fell.

In the following years, Athens battled for ground, while Cleon and Demosthenes, two brilliant Athenian generals, led the charge against Corinth and Sparta. Cleon was a particularly important voice during these years. After the death of Pericles in 429 B.C.E., he stepped up to lead Athens. An advocate for war, he beat the Spartans in battle twice in 425 B.C.E., both at Pylos and Sphacteria (The Editors of Encyclopaedia Britannica, 2020).

However, despite their best efforts, Athens' victories ground to a halt in 424 B.C.E. General Brasidas, Sparta's best strategist at the time, was able to fend off Athenian forces in Megara and Boeotia. Reluctantly, a year of peace was brokered.

In 422 B.C.E., war resumed. Brasidas led Spartan forces against Cleon, who was heading the Athenian army. At Amphipolis, the Spartans won, but Brasidas was killed alongside Cleon.

With the death of two pro-war leaders, Nicias, an Athenian politician and general, was able to negotiate for peace in 421 B.C.E. Called the Peace of Nicias, it was hoped that the war would be brought to a close, or at least to a temporary halt (Bloxham, 2016). Unfortunately, by 418 B.C.E., hostilities resumed. Sparta, led by Agis II, defeated Argos, an ally of Athens. In retaliation, Athens attacked Melos for supporting Sparta.

Around the same time, the Athenian generals Nicias and Demosthenes reluctantly mounted an expedition to Sicily. Alcibiades, a brilliant, wealthy, and well-connected Athenian, who proposed the idea, hoped Sicily might provide resources and allies. The expedition did not go well, ending in the deaths of Nicias and Demosthenes as well as most of their men. Alcibiades, realizing that he'd be blamed, fled Athens. He dwelt in Sparta for a time, acting as a military advisor against his native city. His political connivance made him enemies there, so he later fled to Persia to advise the satrap Tissaphernes until 410 B.C.E., when his friends secured a safe return to Athens.

Athens needed his expertise. In 412 B.C.E., Rhodes had successfully revolted and joined Sparta, and Athens great rival was now led by a fierce new general, Lysander. Yet, Alcibiades led the Athenians to several victories, starting with the Battle of Cyzicus in 410 B.C.E. After more victories around the Aegean,

Alcibiades returned to Athens and accepted the position of *strategos autokrator*, commander of all Athens' forces on land and sea.

However, Sparta was not giving up. It managed to forge an alliance with Persia in 408 B.C.E. Two years later, Lysander beat the Athenian fleet at Notium, near Ephesus. This failure reflected poorly on Alcibiades, and the talented but erratic general was forced again into exile.

When Lysander overwhelmed Athens' forces in 404 B.C.E. at the Battle of Aegospotami, he showed no mercy, executing 3,000 captives. Lysander cut off Athens from its port, Piraeus. He then destroyed its fortifications and laid siege until the starving city was forced to surrender.

With that, Sparta won the war, replacing the Athenian empire with one of its own. However, Sparta's allies, Corinth in particular, had borne the brunt of the war's destruction. Sparta would soon find, as Athens had, that hegemony is difficult to handle.

Effects of the Peloponnesian War

After Sparta's victory and Athens's surrender in 404 B.C.E., the Delian League disbanded. Athens was thrown into disarray. The democratic system briefly collapsed, and "Thirty Tyrants" were appointed by Lysander to keep the city unified. In the chaos, Athenians were killed, pro-democratic citizens were exiled, and private property was confiscated.

While many Athenians still had the right to bear arms, live in the city, and take part in jury trials, the "Thirty Tyrants" became brutal in their punishments. Neutral citizens began to revolt. A revolution transformed the regime, and Athens finally began to rebuild.

Meanwhile, Sparta's power grew. Not only were their naval forces more honed, but they were able to maintain Athens's old hegemony across the Aegean Sea for a time. At one point, they too began to believe they could invade the Persians.

But the relationship between Sparta and its allies deteriorated quickly, and the destroyer of Athenian power entered a war against an alliance of Thebes, Corinth, Athens, and Argos in 395 B.C.E. The "Corinthian War" lasted for 8 years, but the Greek *poleis* were exhausted after more than 40 years of fighting.

In reality, although Sparta came out nominally on top in the conflict, Persia was the real winner. After hostilities ceased in 387 B.C.E., the Persians were free of Greek meddling in Asia Minor. And in 371 B.C.E., at the Battle of Leuctra, the tactical genius of Epaminondas would lead Thebes in the annihilation of Sparta's military supremacy forever (*Effects of the Peloponnesian War*, 2023).

The end of both Sparta and Athens is best illustrated by the fates of their last heroes—Alcibiades and Lysander. Alcibiades, seeking refuge in Persia from Lysander's forces, died around 404 B.C.E., likely murdered by the Persians in Phrygia. Lysander died in 395 B.C.E., in a small skirmish. He led his troops too close to the walls of the *polis* of Haliartus at the start of the Corinthian War. A nearby Theban force moved to assist the city, and Lysander was killed in the melee. Just as their heroes died after falling from glory, neither of the two greatest *poleis* would fully recover after their decades-long quarrel.

The Philosophical Triumvirate: Socrates, Plato, Aristotle

While the Classical Era reached a high point before the Peloponnesian War, some progress was still made after it. This was particularly true in the field of philosophy. Moving beyond spirituality and traditional cult religion, philosophers like Socrates, Plato, and Aristotle began to explore the big questions of life and reality.

While their fields of interest weren't exactly the same, Socrates impacted Plato, who in turn left an impression on Aristotle. These three men formed the all-important foundation for the field of philosophy. It is a foundation that has lasted up to the 21st century.

Socrates: The Only True Wisdom Is Knowing You Know Nothing

The father of philosophy, Socrates, emerged into a world of upheaval and uncertainty. Born in 469 B.C.E. to a moderately wealthy family, Socrates received a good education, studying rhetoric under

Aspasia, Pericles's gifted consort. Despite his interest in his studies, Socrates took part in the Peloponnesian War.

When Socrates returned home, he lived humbly. He tended to move about Athens and talk with people. Barefoot, long-haired, and unwashed, Socrates didn't cut a fine figure in a city that prized beauty above everything else. According to historians, he was not handsome. Socrates was simply more focused on the things he thought were important—discovering truth and exploring ideas about ethics and how to conduct your life.

Always questioning the *status quo*, Socrates talked with people everywhere. He spoke with intellectuals, political leaders, young men, and admiring students. Two of his favored students were Plato, a fellow philosopher, and Xenophon, an historian. They wrote down Socrates's dialogues *Memorabilia*, *Apology*, *Symposium*, and *Crito*, among others.

These works describe how Socrates talked to people. While Plato's *Dialogues* are considered to be accurate, Xenophon's version is often more trusted. This is due to his historically neutral stance on Socrates (Brinkhof, 2022).

Socrates was famous for many reasons. Although Plato and Xenophon never recorded direct speeches from Socrates on what he believed, some inferences can be drawn. From what we can glean, Socrates:

- formulated a new way of learning by using "the Socratic method," asking questions and creating a dialogue between teacher and student (Kruse, 2022).

- focused on logical consistency, definitions, and virtues.

- believed the soul was more important than our physical bodies or the material world.

- encouraged his listeners to care for their souls and consider how to properly develop virtues (Cooper, 1998).

Despite Socrates' interest in the truth, he became embroiled in politics. This drew Meletus' attention to him. Not much is known about Meletus, but in 399 B.C.E., he charged Socrates with showing a lack of piety and corrupting young men.

Although the 70-year-old provided a passionate defense, trying to prove his way of life was actually in service to the gods, the jury found him guilty. Socrates' students tried to turn the punishment into a hefty fine, but Meletus and his supporters managed to swing the vote in favor of execution. In the end, Socrates chose to drink a cup of brewed hemlock (Standjofski, 2022).

According to Plato, the execution was delayed for a month because of a festival. During that time, Socrates' friends encouraged him to run away. Socrates refused.

Instead, when the time arrived, he willingly drank the brewed poison, walked around until he couldn't feel his legs anymore, lay down, and then, over time, died, surrounded by his friends and admirers. Later scholars and scientists have noted that Plato's noble retelling of Socrates' death fails to mention how the hemlock would have slowly paralyzed his lungs and heart, suffocating him to death slowly (History.com Editors, 2009b).

Why did this travesty happen? There are no clear answers as to why Socrates was targeted. Some scholars suggest it was due to conservative religious sentiment. Socrates stated that if people didn't understand what piety and moral virtue truly were, their faith and actions were a sham. That could have upset some people.

Other scholars believe that Socrates had been too critical of the political establishment, particularly Athenian democracy. Socrates was most prolific in the wake of the Peloponnesian War when Athens was in decline and under the rule of the Thirty Tyrants. During this period, Athenians might not have wanted to hear critiques of their ideas or political ideals. Oddly enough, Critias, the leader of the Thirty Tyrants, was a student of Socrates. Despite that, the Thirty Tyrants didn't save Socrates from death.

Regardless, the father of philosophy transformed the world. He caused people to question their values and ideas. He also raised a generation of philosophers, who would propound ideas that echoed through the centuries down to the present.

Plato: Thinking—The Talking of the Soul with Itself

Born around 428 B.C.E. during the Age of Pericles, Plato grew up in a world of transformation and upheaval, much like his mentor and teacher Socrates. He came from a noble family. His father died when he was a child, and his mother remarried a politician. As a result, Plato was afforded the best education, studying philosophy, gymnastics, and poetry under great teachers.

However, the world he grew up in wasn't easy. Plato came of age during the Peloponnesian War, just about when Sparta defeated Athens once and for all. Therefore, as a young man, Plato saw his city torn apart by competing pro-Spartan and pro-Athenian factions. In the midst of it all, Socrates became a voice of wisdom. Plato, drawn to the wise philosopher, became invested in Socrates' ideas.

When Socrates was forced to commit suicide, Plato left Athens and traveled through south Italy, Sicily, and Egypt. Meeting other scholars, scientists, and academics, Plato began to form his own ideas about life, reality, and virtue. He returned to Athens in 387 B.C.E., bought a plot of land outside the city, and started his Academy, a school for philosophical thinking.

In many ways, Plato's Academy is considered to be the world's first university. Plato gave lectures to students who traveled miles to hear him. One student, hailing from northern Greece, was Aristotle, aged 17.

As an academic teacher, Plato was able to formalize his ideas. Throughout his travels and teaching period, Plato came to grips with his own ideas, based on Socrates's concepts. Not only did Plato carry forward and immortalize some of Socrates' words, but he also began to explore his own ideas and push back against the wisdom of his great teacher (History.com Editors, 2009b).

Plato was prolific. In his writings, he:

- provided a defense for Socrates' ideas, pushing back against contemporary criticism and lampooning.

- discussed general topics like the nature of love or the forgotten wisdom of the soul (*Symposium* and *Meno*).

- theorized about the parts of the soul (reason, spirit, and appetite) and linked them to three main groups of a city-state (*The Republic*).

- proposed that the best city-state would be led by a philosopher-king (*The Republic*) (Meinwald, 2018).

- suggested that virtues, such as goodness or beauty, were based in another plane of reality (known as the Theory of Forms, articulated in *Phaedo* and *Parmenides*) (Turner, 1903).

- encouraged readers to dwell on the true forms in order to bring virtue and lost knowledge from our previous lives.

- encouraged readers to create their own path to self-improvement.

- wrote topical discussions on geometry, politics, and general knowledge (Kraut, 2004).

In 347 B.C.E., Plato died of old age and was buried near the Academy. However, his ideas continued to change the world. Not only did he open the world of philosophy to Aristotle, but his Academy would survive in various forms until the 6th century CE.

Although his Academy would shift focus a few times, from dogmatic, speculative, moral-focused thought to skepticism and then Middle Platonism and Neoplatonism, the Academy provided the world with an ongoing font of philosophic thought (The Editors of Encyclopaedia Britannica, 2017b). The Byzantine Empire and Islamic thinkers particularly enjoyed Plato's work, while the West focused on the writings of his most famous student, Aristotle.

Aristotle: Knowing Yourself Is the Beginning of All Wisdom

Aristotle entered a different world from Socrates and Plato. In 384 B.C.E., Aristotle was born in Stagira, located in the north of Greece. At the age of 17, Aristotle was sent south to Athens to study at Plato's Academy, where he learned from Plato himself. After remaining there as both a student and teacher for 20 years, he left the Academy when Plato died. This may have been due either to rising anti-Macedonian sentiment in Athens or Academy politics.

For the next five years, Aristotle traveled along the coast of Asia Minor, staying at Assos and Lesbos where former students housed him. He married, had a daughter, and continued his studies. He also tutored King Philip II of Macedon's son, Alexander, starting in 343 B.C.E.

Returning to Athens by 335 B.C.E., Aristotle started his own school, called The Lyceum. Students from all around the Greek world attended to hear his lectures, take his courses, and use his massive research library. Thanks to Aristotle's wide interests, students at The Lyceum studied a wide array of subjects including various fields of science, rhetoric, literature, theology, and the arts (Shields, 2008).

It was during this period that Aristotle did most of his writing. He supposedly wrote around 200 works, but due to poor storage after his death, only 31 survived. What remained of Aristotle's writings was poorly organized, not chronologically ordered, and very dense. However, many scholars break Aristotle's writings into four basic categories: analytical, theoretical, practical, and rhetorical or literary-focused (History.com Editors, 2019).

Like Plato, Aristotle went through phases. He first defended his teacher's ideas, then analyzed and critiqued them, and finally (after 335 B.C.E.) began to formulate his own philosophy. Aristotle moved from examining the natural world, as seen in his biology, marine biology, and botany treatises, and began to think about more existential and philosophical topics (Haskett et al., 2016). Some ideas that Aristotle considered include:

- ways to carry out scientific or philosophical investigations (*On Interpretation, Prior Analytics*).

- empiricism and how to determine truth with the five senses.

- definitions of logic, logical fallacies, as well as the aims and role of logic.

- writings on cosmology, physics, metaphysics, and animals.

- treatises on ethics and politics (*Nicomachean Ethics, Politics*).

- a defense of the role, aim, and therapeutic benefits of literature (*Poetics*).

- explanations on how to create logical syllogism (arguments) with two premises and a conclusion sentence (*Dialectics*).

- exploration of the definitions and techniques of persuasion (*Rhetoric*).

- a proposal that "a good life" is discovered by understanding and fulfilling your individual, unique function, pursuing virtuous living, embracing reason, and achieving some comfort and pleasures in life.

- the definition of different political states, in which he reluctantly supports polity (majority of people ruling in the interest of all) as having the most long-term success.

- the importance of proper environments for individual personal growth.

- defense of humanity's natural tendency to hierarchies.

- a study on nature, being, function, and substance, with a focus on the importance of classification as a way to define and understand the world around us.

- a definition of *telos* (your purpose in life) and the role it plays in helping you understand your function and your path to "the good life."

It is important to note that by focusing on function, on different types of life, and the naturalization of hierarchies, Aristotle became a springboard for justifying unhealthy cultural practices, such as slavery and the unequal treatment of women. Although Aristotle did believe that nonliving machines would one day replace slaves, ideas about "natural" slaves would come into play as justification for slavery centuries later, particularly among the conquistadors (Messerly, 2014).

As he aged, Aristotle faced the usual challenges of life. His wife passed away, and Aristotle found love again with a woman called Herpyllis, who some say was a servant in his home. Herpyllis and Aristotle had a son, Nicomachus, after whom he named his famous treatise, the Nicomachean Ethics. However, after tensions rose between the Greeks and Macedonians, Aristotle fled Athens. A year later, in 322 B.C.E., he died of natural causes.

Following his death, Aristotle's Lyceum, failing to compete adequately against Plato's Academy, collapsed. Aristotle's writings, poorly stored away, were forgotten. Andronicus of Rhodes rescued them in 30 B.C.E. After grouping and editing what he could collect, copies were maintained. Aristotle's works would become popular in Byzantium, the Islamic World, and, centuries later, in medieval Europe (History.com Editors, 2019).

Like his teachers, the importance of Aristotle cannot be underestimated. Not only did he become one of the world's first documented scientists, but he also formalized the identity of scientific disciplines like botany and marine biology. Among the Greeks, Aristotle was the first professor to organize lectures into a course and create a syllabus for his students. His research library was renowned for its accumulated knowledge, which helped preserve the advancements of the era. In this way, the lineage of critical thinking and questioning would be preserved from well beyond the age of the three greatest Greek philosophers.

When the Dust Settles

Despite the great achievements of Athens and the might of Sparta, the city-states could not weather the storm of clashing ambition. Greece had managed to fend off the Persians, proving to the known world that they were a military power to be reckoned with. However, the fall of Athens and Sparta signaled a time of radical transformation.

As the smoke of the Peloponnesian Wars cleared, a new power emerged in the north, ready to change the course of Greek history forever. Chapter 6 will explore the rise of Macedon and the remarkable figure who would go on to conquer the known world.

Part 3: The Rise of Macedon and the Hellenistic Period

Chapter 6: The Rise of Macedon

> I swear this oath by Zeus, Gaia, Helios, Posei-
> don, Athena, Ares, and all the gods and
> goddesses. I shall abide in peace and not break
> these covenants. Neither shall I bear arms
> against any who likewise swear, either on land
> or sea... nor shall I seek to end the dominion of
> Philip and his progeny. (IG II² 236)

These are the words of the oath given to the League of Corinth, formed by an unusual man— Philip II of Macedon. The mercurial rise of this Macedonian king is a thrilling story of a man driven by ambition, bolstered by success, and destroyed by his own appetites. In his 23-year reign, Philip did what none had managed before him—unify Macedonia and Greece.

How did a kingdom in the northern fringes of Greece rise to dominate the entire Hellenic world in such a short span of time? To most Greeks, the Macedonians were no better than other barbarians, even though they spoke a rough dialect of Greek. The answer lies in the figure of Philip himself. His ambitions drove him to extend his territory on the battlefield and at the negotiating table.

Despite his detractors, Philip cultivated diplomatic relations with the Greek *poleis*, provided refuge at his capital city of Pela for great thinkers, and charmed those who met him. He drank hard, fought hard, and lived hard. In many ways, Philip was the rock'n'roll star of his era (Griffith, 2019).

Philip II

Born in Aegae in 382 B.C.E., the youngest of three sons, Philip II was ushered into a world of upheaval and uncertainty. His father, King Amyntas III of Macedonia, ruled a struggling realm. Macedonia would one day grow to include the modern-day Republic of North Macedonia, northern Greece, and parts of Bulgaria, Albania, Serbia, and Kosovo. However, during Phillip's youth, his country was not unified.

Early Career

When the Greeks of Thebes invaded Macedon, they captured the teenage Philip and took him hostage. Living there for three years, he studied under the Greeks. Epaminondas, the great Theban general who had crushed the Spartans at Leuctra in 371 B.C.E., taught Philip about military strategy. The Macedonian was a quick study.

After he returned home, Philip initially helped his second oldest brother, Perdiccas III, rule (his oldest brother had died). When Perdiccas died in battle fighting Illyrians in modern-day Albania, Philip deposed his nephew and took the Macedonian throne at the age of 23.

The first thing Philip focused on was stabilizing Macedonia. It wasn't easy. Relying on a cunning combination of threats and warfare, Philip managed to secure the loyalty of both the core Macedonian nobility and many of the barons of outlying hill regions.

Macedonia, compared to Greece, was not as advanced technologically or culturally. However, Philip saw his people's hidden potential. He believed his family's lineage traced back to Heracles, son of Zeus, so he was determined to prove the royal family's worth.

The new king invested in bringing culture to Macedon's capital city, Pella. Philip invited philosophers and writers to stay. Aristotle was hired to teach

Philip's son Alexander for a couple of years. Philip cultivated Pella as a center of culture and diplomacy.

Philip's Military Innovations

One of the keys to Philip's success was his military prowess. By listening to his tutors, such as the experienced general Epaminondas, Philip was not only able to transform the Macedonian army, but he was also able to pioneer strategies that surprised his Greek opponents.

The first step Philip tackled was the transformation of the Macedonian army. Under Philip, Macedon's army increased from 10,000 to 24,000 men. The cavalry was boosted from a royal guard of 600 to a battalion of 3,500. Philip introduced many other reforms to help increase his military power, including (*The Military Revolution: What Were Philip II's Reforms of the Macedonian Military and How Revolutionary Were They?*, n.d.):

- an oath of allegiance.

- well-made gear and uniforms.

- strict training exercises for improved fitness, including forced marches.

- regular drills to increase tactical flexibility and unit cohesion.

- a fair punishment and reward system.

- allowances for restricted looting.

- good, regular pay.

- education and training in Greek military techniques and strategy.

- a new weapon—the *sarissa* (a 13 to 23-foot-long pike).

- practice in multiple forms of weaponry, including the sarissa, swords, and bows.

- new siege weaponry including towers, catapults, and battering rams.

Philip took care to account for several different types of warfare as he reformed his military apparatus. The Persians had relied on long-range weapons like bows and slings to soften their enemies before charging with heavy lancers and other cavalry. For them, most infantry was poorly armored, but mobile. On the other hand, the Greeks had shown the effectiveness of a heavily armored hoplite phalanx in holding position or attacking straight ahead, especially if its flanks were protected. Philip doubled down on the offensive power of the phalanx, replacing the shorter hoplite spear with the sarissa and reducing his phalangites' armor (Wasson, 2014).

Philip's heavy infantry soldiers were not perfect, however. The phalanx, despite its immense mass and forward impetus, could sometimes struggle on uneven terrain. Moreover, these formations could be easily flanked since larger phalanxes couldn't turn quickly. And while the sarissa was able to fend off oncoming attacks, if the formation lost cohesion and the enemy closed in, the phalangites' sarissa was less wieldy than short swords or smaller spears (Roman Legionary, Macedonian Phalanx, or Spartan Hoplite: Which Was the Better Ancient Warrior?, 2023). Philip's answer was a combined arms approach.

He outfitted an elite corps of infantry called the *pezhetairoi* or "foot-companions." They were highly-trained professionals chosen for their size, strength, and facility with multiple weapons. Scholars debate whether they carried the sarissa or a shorter one-handed spear, but the prominent placement of the *pezhetairoi* at crucial places on the battle line is testimony to the importance Philip placed upon them.

In addition, Philip maintained both light and heavy cavalry squadrons and recruited poorer citizens as javelineers and other light infantry. With these additions, the heavy phalanx formed the iron core of a flexible force capable of operating on any terrain against nearly any opponent. It would lay the foundation for Macedonian power in the age of Philip and beyond.

Eventually, with his new army, Philip subdued the Illyrians, completely defeating them in 359 B.C.E. Then, Philip turned his eye toward his next concern—

Athens. Athens controlled nearby silver and gold mines, and the major city-state was also interfering in Macedonian politics. Philip captured Amphipolis in 357 B.C.E., took its gold and silver mines from Athens, and then moved to capture other *poleis*.

The Unification of Greece

Philip II was invested in stabilizing Macedon and its diplomatic relationships in order to enlarge its territory. But after he captured Amphipolis, Crenides (which he renamed to Philippi), and other city-states, the fragmented Greek *poleis* united against him. However, Philip proved himself adept at leveraging the ongoing divisions among the Greeks.

In 354 or 353 B.C.E., the Thessalian League, a loose confederation of northern Greek *poleis*, asked Philip for help fighting Phocis and its allies, including Athens and Sparta, in the Third Sacred War over the holy sanctuary of Delphi. Philip agreed.

The Greek city-states were cautious about entering open battle. Nevertheless, Philip defeated Phocis and its allies several times, most notably in the Battle of Crocus Field in 353 or 352 B.C.E. Philip's victory saw him named *archon* of Thessalian League, giving him full authority over the considerable army and revenue of Thessaly. Neither side claimed a complete victory, but Philip came out of the Third Sacred War more powerful than he went in. The Athenians took over the pass of Thermopylae barring Philip from pressing into central and southern Greece.

Philip opted to negotiate over the next six years. As the newly installed *archon* of the Thessalian League, he was able to negotiate a long-term alliance with the Greeks. Despite his capture of more cities and having proven his military might, Philip preferred to find a peaceful resolution between himself and Athens.

Demosthenes, a famous Athenian orator, hated Philip. He constantly warned his fellow Athenians about the danger that the Macedonian king represented. His eloquent venom was such that, to this day, an exceptionally bitter verbal denunciation is called a philippic. Yet, during the lengthy diplomatic maneuvering, Philip continued to expand wherever possible. He annexed Thrace to the east, tightened his hold on Thessaly, and completely took over Illyria.

The Greeks, at length, realizing Demosthenes was right, reopened the war against Philip in 339 B.C.E. They swayed the once-friendly Thebes to their side. Nevertheless, the Battle of Chaeronea in August of 338 B.C.E. settled the matter of Greece's independence for the foreseeable future.

Philip and his 18-year-old son Alexander III crushed a large army of 35,000 formed by Athens, Thebes, Corinth, and several other powerful *poleis*. With a resounding victory, Philip showed his overwhelming supremacy on the battlefield. He then forced a peace treaty that ensured support from the Greeks going forward.

The victory at Chaeronea put Philip in a position to expand the borders of his territory, unite the city-states of Greece into a new political body, and begin planning an expedition to capture the riches of the east. Securing his position in Greece with garrisons in Thebes and Corinth, Philip still needed to tackle the more sensitive issue of how to handle Athens. Without Athens, he couldn't hope to take on Persia.

As a result, in 337 B.C.E., Philip created the League of Corinth, also called the Hellenic League. This organization was formed to help preserve peace between the city-states within the League as well as with Macedon. Most of the Greek island colonies and almost all the city-states on the mainland supported the alliance. Sparta was the most notable exception.

The League's guiding principle was war with Persia in revenge for its invasions of the previous century. For the first time in history, the city-states of Greece (*sans* Sparta) were united under a single political organization. With Philip in power, the city-states would not only behave, but they could rely on Philip's forces combined with Athens's navy to provide proper protection for everyone.

Every city-state had a representative at the *synedrion*, or congress. The only exception was Macedon, since Philip was the head, or *hegemon*, of the League and looked after his homeland's interests. This council decided on matters that best worked to the city-states' advantage. As part of the League, each *polis* was required to provide ships or troops. The amount required depended on their power.

Thanks to Philip's diplomacy and military prowess, Macedon was positioned at the head of large collection of powerful city-states. It had the combined strength, resources, and wisdom of the Greek *poleis*. Unwillingly, Greece had been united, but it was this important step that would lead to the creation of the first, true Hellenic Empire (Griffith, 2019).

Preparing for Empire

If Philip wanted to achieve his dream of taking on the might of Persia, he would need as many allies as possible. The Greeks had formidable armies, a long history of military victories, and academic resources that would provide Philip with the foundation he needed for empire-building. Recognizing that he couldn't do it all on his own, Philip set about to form alliances. Through the League of Corinth, as well as his own marriages, Philip was able to build a robust network of shared interests.

The League of Corinth

The League of Corinth, as noted above, was established later in Philip's life. Formed after years of warfare and treaties, the League represented the first tangible progress toward unifying Greece and consolidating Philip's power. Initially proposed by Isocrates of Athens in 346 B.C.E., it took years to form. However, it was the first politically unifying institution in

Greek history and paved the way for future expansion.

There were three parts to the League of Corinth. In addition to Philip the *hegemon* and the *synedrion* council were the *dikastai*, important judges who aided in decision-making. When decrees were made, they were posted to cities such as Athens, Corinth, Olympia, and Delphi (Chrysopoulos, 2023a).

As part of joining the League, each *polis* swore an oath, stating they would keep the peace, bear arms for their allies, and uphold Philip's position. They also promised punishment for any signatory who violated the oath, stating, "But should any oathbreaker violate these covenants, I shall assist those in need however they demand, and I shall wage war upon the transgressor however the council and *hegemon* (i.e. Philip) should command me" (IG II³,1 318).

Therefore, this council of Greeks decided on major military and political moves and represented the military and naval power of each *polis* proportionately. City-states with less military power were represented less, but they still had a voice at the table. When the first meeting was held, Philip was able to successfully negotiate support from the League in pursuit of war with Persia. Philip was, of course, elected as the chief commander of the armed forces, the *strategos autokrator* (The Editors of Encyclopædia Britannica, 2020).

The Marriages of Philip II

Diplomacy, peace treaties, and the formation of the League weren't the only ways Philip gathered support; Philip was also open to marriages, many of them. Although the chronology of his unions is not certain, how they supported his ambitions for power and territory can be surmised. Each of these women hailed from different regions or cities, and their marriages to Philip more than likely coincided with the acquisition of new territory (Tronson, 1984):

- Audata: from Illyria, bore Cynane (daughter).

- Phila: from Elimeia, no children.

- Philinna: from Larissa, bore Arrhidaeus (son).

- Olympias: from Epirus, bore Alexander (son) and Cleopatra (daughter).

- Meda: from Thrace, no children.

- Nicesipolis: from Thessaly, bore Thessalonika (daughter).

- Cleopatra: from Macedonia, bore Europa (daughter) and Caranus (son).

The two most famous wives of Philip were undoubtedly Olympias and Cleopatra. Olympias was
the mother of Alexander III. She was a wise and powerful woman, manipulative and capable. Long after
Philip's death, through their son, Alexander, her cunning helped shape the fate of nations.

Cleopatra, on the other hand, was young when
she married Philip. She was chosen to bear Philip a
true heir with "pure" Macedonian blood. The young
woman bore Philip a son, directly threatening Alexander's inheritance. This circumstance enraged
Olympias and set things in motion that would un-
leash the greatest conqueror the world had ever seen
(Mann, 2013).

Philip's Final Years

When Philip formed the League of Corinth in 337 B.C.E., Persia was calling. But before he could achieve that dream, personal issues erupted in the warrior-king's personal life. Alexander's intelligence and ambition matched Philip's, sometimes raising tension between the two high-spirited men. Furthermore, Alexander's birth was not considered "pure" enough for the Macedonian throne.

To solve this issue, Philip took the advice of his close friend and commander, Attalus. Therefore, also in 337 B.C.E., Philip married his seventh wife, Cleopatra, the niece of Attalus. She was much younger than Philip, and the marriage made Alexander angry. When Alexander spoke out about it, he and his mother were separated and temporarily exiled. Alexander was sent to Illyria, his mother back to Epirus.

Hoping to properly secure his throne and lineage, personal issues continued to threaten his legacy. Philip's former friend, bodyguard, and (some say) lover, Pausanius of Orestis stabbed him to death during the wedding ceremony of his daughter, Princess Cleopatra. Thus, Philip II died in 336 B.C.E., never fulfilling his dream of conquering Persia and leaving his throne empty for an ambitious son with a destiny that would overshadow his own (Wasson, 2014).

Imperial Premonitions

The year was 344 B.C.E. The evening sun cast long shadows over the grand court of Pella. Philip II of Macedon took his ease and watched his 12-year-old son, Alexander, practicing combat moves with sheer determination. The boy's relentless spirit was evident even at this age. It wasn't just training for battle, but a dance of aspiration. That is what Philip saw: a dream. Every stroke of the sword promised an empire larger than any the world had seen.

With that ambition, Philip unified Greece. But it was this young prince, with fire in his eyes and ambition in his heart, who redefined the very notion of empire, pushing the boundaries of the known world. He faced the might of Persia and ventured into the mysterious lands of India.

Everywhere he went, he spread the telltale marks of Greek culture, intertwining them with local customs. But more than his conquests, his true legacy was a merging of civilizations—an era of Hellenization. In the next chapter, we journey alongside Alexander, not just as a conqueror, but as a catalyst for the fusion of East and West.

Chapter 7: Alexander the Great and the Hellenization of the East

Many men had tried to ride Bucephalus. None succeeded. Alexander, however, fell in love with the magnificent horse, admiring his ferocity and beauty. Despite his youth, he knew he could tame the noble Thessalian beast before him.

Approaching Bucephalus, the sharp-eyed 12-year-old boy noticed that the horse was afraid of his own shadow. He spoke soothingly, coaxing the black charger toward the sun. Alexander tamed the now calm Bucephalus and would keep him as his prized steed for the next 18 years. His determination, cleverness, and keen eyes had won the day. It was a sign of things to come.

Bucephalus and Alexander fought many battles together. It wasn't until 326 B.C.E. that they parted, when Bucephalus succumbed to wounds taken in the heroic crossing of the Hydaspes river in India. Grieving the loss of his dear friend, Alexander founded a city called Bucephala in honor of the horse who had borne him over 3,500 miles from home.

The story of Alexander and Bucephalus has become famous over the centuries. It isn't just about a boy who loved his horse. It also reveals the core of a man who created an empire (*Bucephalus: The True*

Story of Alexander the Great's Legendary Horse, 2023).

Capable of greatness, generosity, love, ruthlessness, and cruelty, Alexander III of Macedon put his mark on history. Following in his father's footsteps, Alexander achieved the imperial dreams that Philip had harbored. He created an empire stretching from Greece to Egypt, to the Middle East, and beyond to northern India. In the process, he laid the foundation of Hellenistic culture and laid the groundwork for future empires.

Education and Relationships

Alexander, son of King Philip II and his fourth wife, Olympias, was born in 356 B.C.E. into a world where opportunity—and challenge—waited. As the legitimate son of the king of Macedon, Alexander had a warrior for a father and role model. This was reflected by his upbringing, which was characterized by a blend of military, academic, and artistic education. Alexander's curriculum was designed to form a well-rounded man.

Under Leonidas of Epirus, one of his mother's relatives, Alexander learned how to ride a horse, fight, and march long distances. His early training under Leonidas transformed Alexander into a powerful warrior with stamina and resilience.

Lysimachus of Acarnania taught Alexander how to read, write, and play the lyre. Thanks to Lysimachus, Alexander gained a lifelong appreciation of the arts, and spent much of his spare time reading – even when at war. When Alexander was around 13 years old, Philip hired Aristotle to tutor him.

During Alexander's youth, he made important friends who impacted his life in positive and negative ways. Some of his childhood friends were Cassander, Callisthenes, and Hephaestion. This last was particularly close to Alexander, becoming his second-in-command and most trusted confidant. Many historians have debated the relationship between Alexander and his boyhood friend, but what is known is that Hephaestion remained at Alexander's side until the end of his life (Mark, 2013).

Eventually, Alexander grew up. Like his father before him, Alexander brokered marriages for political and personal reasons. Alexander's polygamy was not as extensive as his father's; he married three times, once for love (Roxana, a Sogdian princess in 327 B.C.E.) and twice for politics (the Persian princesses Stateira and Parysatis in 324 B.C.E.). Roxana and Stateira were particularly powerful consorts who vied for influence after the death of Alexander (Edwards, 2022).

Outside his marriages, Alexander had several possible lovers, including the Thessalian woman Campaspe and the Greco-Persian noblewoman Barsine. The latter was a daughter of the Persian satrap of Phrygia and wife of the famous Greek mercenary Memnon of Rhodes, one of Alexander's greatest adversaries.

Alexander may also have had intimate relationships with the men of his inner circle. He was particularly distraught at the death of Hephaestion, but there are no clear references to a sexual relationship in the ancient sources. Likewise, the Persian eunuch Bagoas, who had been a favorite of the emperor Darius III, was a member of Alexander's Persian court. The ancient sources describe an episode where Alexander was drunk at a festival and kissed Bagoas at the urging of the other Macedonians.

Unfortunately, modern inferences about the sexuality of ancient figures are largely doomed to failure. Primarily, these exercises illustrate the preoccupations of modern scholars more than those of the ancients. Furthermore, even if we could determine with any certainty the social constructs within which ancient sexuality operated (a dubious claim), the sources at our disposal rarely offer enough material to analyze against them. The best we can do is reaffirm what the sources state explicitly: Alexander married three times, had a few love affairs with prominent women, and may have enjoyed similar relationships with a select group of men.

Alexander's Conquests

Alexander began his career on the battlefield at an early age. At 18, he helped Philip win the Battle of Chaeronea by commanding the left wing of the Macedonian battle line. Upon Philip's assassination, the 20-year-old Alexander took the throne and began to work on his own plans for building an empire.

Starting in Thessaly and Thrace, Alexander revisited old territory, ensuring his power was secure in the north. For the rest of Greece, he used Thebes as a warning, razing the once might *polis* to the ground while keeping its temples intact. Athens and other city-states got the message, allowing Alexander to conquer much of Greece and form a strong foundation for his future conquests.

The Battle of the Granicus

In 334 B.C.E., Alexander crossed into Persia. At first, it wasn't easy to maintain a foothold. The Battle of the Granicus was the first great test of Alexander's mettle, and that of the allied Macedonian and Greek army.

His 40,000 men met an equally large force commanded by Arsites, the satrap of Phrygia, on opposite sides of the Granicus River. The armies were fairly well-balanced. So, victory was determined by how well the men were led, whether the army was able to act as a unit, and how disciplined the soldiers were.

Alexander knew he would make for easy bait. Deliberately choosing clothing that stood out, Alexander drew most of the attacks toward his own unit. This involved him in heavy fighting.

According to Arrian, our most reliable source for the battle, Alexander spotted Mithridates, one of Emperor Darius' sons-in-law, and killed him with a spear thrust to the face. However, Rhosaces, one of Darius' satraps, struck Alexander on the helmet with his sword. The young Macedonian king was unbowed and ran the Persian through the chest with his spear.

Another satrap, Spithridates, maneuvered to strike Alexander from behind, but his companion, Cleitus the Black, hewed off the satrap's arm, rescuing his king. The death of so many Persian commanders, Alexander's survival, and the steady pressure of the Macedonian phalangites eventually caused the Persians to rout (Bileta, 2023). Alexander had defeated the only imperial army then in Asia Minor.

For the next year, Alexander fought to pacify the cities of Asia Minor. The Persian fleet was still operating in the Aegean, and he needed to deny them safe ports. Some cities surrendered without a fight, others he needed to take by assault. Nevertheless, his boundless energy enabled Alexander to exert control over most of the region within a year.

The Battle of Issus

In 333 B.C.E., Alexander faced off against King Darius in person. Darius tried to approach the battle with Alexander more strategically than his satraps had the year before. By careful maneuvering, he split Alexander's army, forcing the Macedonian and his men to march over 60 miles in two days to rejoin with one another. Arriving at Issus, Alexander knew his force of 40,000 men was outnumbered by King Darius' army nearly two to one.

The warlords faced each other across the Pinarus River where it met the coast. Alexander deployed his Greek Thessalian cavalry on the left wing, near to the seashore and under command of Parmenion, one of his father's most trusted generals. They stood opposite the more numerous Persian heavy lancers. The phalanx held the middle, opposite a large body of heavily armed Greek mercenaries on Darius' payroll. Alexander himself led his heavy companion cavalry and light infantry on the right wing. They faced off against Persian heavy and light infantry that greatly overextended the Macedonian line. Darius and his bodyguard commanded the Persians from the middle.

The Persian heavy cavalry crossed the river to attack the Thessalians *en masse,* but the Greeks stood firm, buying time under the stalwart Parmenion. The right half of Alexander's phalanx crossed to the Persian side but suffered heavy losses against the hardened Greek mercenaries and had to retreat. Meanwhile, Alexander dismounted and led a force of hypaspists ("shield bearers") to drive a wedge into the Persian line and relieve pressure from his exhausted phalangites. The maneuver successfully opened a gap in the Persian line.

The king re-mounted Bucephalus and led a charge into the gap while his javelineers held off the Persian enveloping force on his right. He completely pierced the formation of the enemy and forced Darius's army into retreat. King Darius himself panicked and fled the scene, leaving his army to flounder. Alexander not only beat the king's army, but he also captured King Darius's wife, mother, and two of his daughters (Bileta, 2023).

The Siege of Tyre

Before going eastward, Alexander consolidated his territory in Syria and Phoenicia, still seeking to neutralize the Persian navy by denying it safe harbors in Asia Minor and the Levant. To that end, in 332

B.C.E., Alexander laid siege to Tyre, a large Phoenician port. This city was important because it was the major base for King Darius's navy.

However, it was not easy to take. All of the women and children had been sent away to Carthage, an ancient colony of Tyre, leaving only strong defenders behind its massive 150-foot walls. Around 40,000 men defended the city, and they settled in for a long siege.

Alexander decided that he needed to build a huge causeway to reach the city walls across the channel that protected it. It wasn't easy, but eventually, Alexander's engineers managed to build siege towers that could withstand Tyre's missiles and a massive land bridge that brought Alexander's armies to the wall. However, without control of the sea, he could not fully blockade the city.

Fortunately, his diligent capture of ports from Asia Minor to Syria gave him control of their navies. More and more squadrons arrived during the course of the siege. In addition, the king of Cyprus sent a fleet to assist him. Within seven months, Tyre fell. It is estimated that 8,000 men were killed and around 30,000 men were sold into slavery. The surrender and occupation of Tyre were considered a massive victory and an indicator of Alexander's power (Bileta, 2023).

The Liberation of Egypt

The next year, Alexander took control of Egypt, which the Persians had conquered in 525 B.C.E. The Macedonian king sought legitimacy; therefore, he restored many of the Egyptian temples that the Persians had let fall into disrepair. He visited the famous oracle of Amun-Ra at Siwa, where he was proclaimed the son of Amun. He commissioned new temples and reduced the tax burden. On the coast, he founded the city of Alexandria, perhaps his greatest cultural achievement. Finally, he was crowned pharaoh with the traditional Egyptian double crown. Now, with control of the eastern Mediterranean and the entire coast, Alexander was ready to take on the rest of the Persian Empire. But Darius was busy raising new armies in the east to check his advance.

The Battle of Gaugamela

The Battle of Gaugamela (sometimes called Arbela) in 331 B.C.E. was Darius' last chance to keep his empire. He chose the time and place carefully—the flat terrain of the Nineveh Plains of northern Iraq. He ordered the entire battlefield to be cleared of debris to give his huge cavalry and scythed chariot contingents freedom of movement. He then formed up his lines to urge a night battle. However, Alexander waited until morning, allowing his men to rest while the Persians waited up all night in fear of attack.

It's impossible to determine the Persian numbers. The only thing modern scholars agree on is that the ancient sources are wholly unreliable on this point. Unfortunately, modern estimates are hardly more useful, since they vary from 50,000 to 250,000. We can observe the same phenomenon in most reconstructions of ancient battles. In any case, every source, ancient and modern, affirms that the Persians hugely outnumbered Alexander, who had about 30,000 heavy infantry, 9,000 light infantry, and 7,000 mixed cavalry.

The width of the Persian line exceeded Alexander's by nearly a mile, making envelopment almost a certainty. Nevertheless, the Macedonian chose to attack a numerically superior force head-on across open terrain while at a disadvantage in cavalry. A full examination of the battle reveals the nature of Alexander's generalship.

He drew up a double battle line. His Macedonian phalanx formed the center, while his lighter infantry, skirmishers, and cavalry took the wings. The second line was a phalanx of mixed Greek allies and native auxiliaries. As the battle unfolded, Alexander would command the entire right half of the line, while Parmenion oversaw the left.

Alexander ordered his Macedonian phalanx forward to engage the Persian center, keeping his light infantry and cavalry forces echeloned back. Darius knew that his infantry was no match for the phalangites head-to-head. Therefore, he committed his center to a holding action and sent an overwhelming cavalry force and his heaviest infantry to outflank and annihilate Parmenion. He hoped a crushing blow would allow his forces to roll up the Macedonian line from the left, neutralizing the moral effect of Alexander.

But the young king wasted no time and led the Companions sharply to the right, extending the Macedonian line in an apparent move to flank the much larger Persian army. As he neared the edge of the territory Darius had cleared for the battle, the Persian king ordered cavalry opposite Alexander to engage, preventing the Macedonian from reaching terrain where the Persian mobility advantage would dissipate.

What followed was an intense cavalry skirmish in which Alexander proved himself one of the great battlefield captains in history. With judicious use of his tactical reserves, incredible discipline, and a willingness to expose himself to physical danger, his mix of cavalry and light foot skirmishers forced the Persian horse to withdraw.

In response, Darius ordered his 200 scythed chariots to engage Alexander directly. However, Alexander moved up the Agrianians, elite javelineers from the Balkans, to screen the Companions. The skirmishers effectively disrupted the chariots who ineffectively drove through lanes in the Macedonian formation. As they emerged in the Macedonian rear, the Companions' horse grooms and a formation of hypaspists annihilated them.

As the Persians committed more and more men to outflank Alexander, he steadily fed new battalions from his second line into the fray. Eventually, a gap opened between the Persian center, still fighting to hold off the Macedonian phalanx, and the forces trying to outflank Alexander's right. The Macedonian king had lured the Persians.

Alexander formed up the Companions into a wedge, putting every man he could spare behind them. Then, he urged Bucephalus forward into the breach in the Persian line, straight at Darius himself. The Persian royal guard and Greek mercenaries guarding the Great King could not withstand the charge, and the front of the Persian center could not help, it was fully engaged with the Macedonian phalanx. Darius panicked and fled, and most of the Persian reserve lines fled with him.

Alexander wanted to pursue and capture Darius, but he received word that Parmenion was finally being overwhelmed by the main Persian offensive after a stalwart delaying action. Choosing to preserve his army, Alexander attacked the troops surrounding Parmenion from behind in a brutal cavalry strike. 60 Companions were killed, and Hephaestion was seriously wounded. But the Persians were eventually beaten back and routed from the field.

Alexander wasn't able to kill the king, but his army smashed Darius's forces and credibility. The Macedonian king's masterclass in battlefield tactics, discipline in command, trust in his subordinates, physical bravery, and unyielding energy all approached the superhuman at Gaugamela, allowing him to defeat a much larger force in open battle with every disadvantage (Bileta, 2023). If Alexander had fought no other battle in his career, we would still consider Gaugamela one of the greatest displays of combat leadership in history. Yes, King Darius escaped again, but his own men were fed up with their monarch. Darius was murdered by one of his generals, leaving Alexander in control of Persia.

To the East

By 327 B.C.E., Alexander spent 4 years eliminating remaining Persian resistance, pacifying peoples that threatened to leave the empire in the chaos of Darius' demise, and even expanding beyond the reach of any Great King before him. As he conquered more territory, he founded many cities, usually naming them after himself.

He married Roxana, a Sogdian princess reputed to be the most beautiful woman in Asia. He also began to embrace the Persian way of life. Not only did he adopt the Persian style of governance, but he also began to wear Persian clothing and enforce Persian court customs. The custom of *proskynesis*, lying fully prostrate before the king, particularly upset the Macedonians. They felt such a display was suitably only for the gods.

By this time, not everyone was happy with Alexander. Even as he planned to take India, the young conqueror had to deal with mutinous troops. He also began to fear conspiracies against his life. Some threats were real, but some were imagined, making him an unreliable and ruthless ruler.

Eventually, in 326 B.C.E., Alexander reached India. In a hard-fought battle at the Hydaspes River, Alexander outwitted the warrior-king Porus to force a crossing during a stormy night, smashed through a numerically superior advance force, and finally defeated Porus' main force. In the battle, Bucephalus was mortally wounded. Showing clemency, Alexander appointed Porus as satrap, letting him rule the territory over which he had been king, and even enlarging his domain.

At the Hyphasis, his tired army revolted. Forced back, Alexander tried to consolidate his territory, fuse the Persian and Greek cultures, and manage his empire. In many ways, the relatively young man had reached the zenith of his powers, but his happiness did not last long.

In 324 B.C.E., Alexander's best friend, Hephaestion, died. Alexander was overcome with grief. Stories tell of him clinging on to the corpse of his friend until his advisers and other companions dragged him away. After giving his fallen friend a funeral fit for a king, Alexander returned to Babylon.

A year later, on June 13, 323 B.C.E., Alexander fell ill. His life of soldiering, drinking, and feasting finally caught up with him, perhaps. He may also have fallen prey to malaria. Poison is also not out of the question. There is no certainty about what actually happened to Alexander. It is only known that after a night of feasting and drinking, he became sick and died. He was only 32 years old (The Editors of Encyclopædia Britannica, 2021).

Controversies

Although many ancient Greek writers paint Alexander the Great as an incredible warrior and leader, there are accounts—Greek, Roman, and Persian—that hint at a more complex picture. There was a dark side to Alexander. Paranoid, prone to bursts of temper, fanatical, and megalomaniacal, Alexander had a firm belief in his right to rule and wasn't afraid to enforce it. In the earliest days of his kingship, Alexander and his mother likely killed Philip's new wife and her baby daughter. After that, Alexander held to a path that made him a charismatic leader who was equally ruthless and generous. (Gabriel, 2017)

Many stories have been told about Alexander's ruthless, insensitive, harsh, and cruel behavior. Among other things, Alexander was said to have:

- had the eunuch Betis dragged to death behind a chariot after Alexander conquered the city of Gaza.

- burned down the city of Persepolis during a drunken victory celebration after the Battle of Gaugamela.

- killed his friend Cleitus the Black in a drunken rage over an argument.

- imprisoned his childhood friend Callisthenes, who died in prison.

- slaughtered an entire town as a sacrifice for Hephaestion's funeral.

In some cases, Alexander regretted his drunken behavior. His grief after killing Cleitus appeared genuine. However, some of the reasons behind the revolt against Alexander as he headed further into India are interesting. Notably, his army no longer supported him due to his behavior.

With the loss of Hephaestion, Alexander became a loose cannon. While he had always drunk and taken drug-like substances, his abuse became worse after the death of Hephaestion. Instead of holding to a more reliable and wiser lifestyle, Alexander became reckless, stubborn, and impulsive (Jarus & Gordon, 2017).

How did Alexander end up this way? Theories abound. Alexander may have believed the prophesies and rumors about his divinity. He may also have been psychologically troubled or chronically overstressed. Perhaps he missed the support of his mother who had not joined him on his campaigns. The death of Hephaestion clearly caused further distress, as well.

However, some suggest that Alexander never felt confident, despite his charisma and charm. His own lineage had been brought into question by his father. His early education under Aristotle was also more Athenian and, therefore, more cerebral than a normal Macedonian boys' education.

Furthermore, Alexander was depicted as being average (or shorter than average) in height and having other less robust physical characteristics. Other descriptions, coinage portraits, and sculptured busts depict him as being fair-skinned and beardless, pointing to more feminine features.

Even more interestingly, although Alexander enjoyed the company of women, married, and had children, he was very controlled about his sexual encounters. His own mother allegedly pushed him into his first intimate relationship with the Thessalian courtesan, Callixeina. This points to a deeply sensitive or reserved nature, which might not have been initially suited for sustained imperial warfare.

Therefore, Alexander may have been plagued by deep-seated doubts. He needed the support of his mother and close friends. As paranoia caused him to lash out, he undercut the foundations that he relied upon. After the death of his closest and dearest friend, Hephaestion, it was only a matter of time before Alexander, too, would collapse (Gabriel, 2017).

The Legacy of Alexander

Alexander wasn't a perfect person. Even in the eyes of his own people, the young conqueror was a walking contradiction. He pursued war and fulfilled his father's ambitions, but he also loved music and books. He was paranoid and trusted few, but the ones he loved and lost, he grieved deeply. Similarly, while his cruelty is easily tallied, so are the legacies he left behind.

The first major impact of Alexander was the final destruction of the Persian Empire. While Persian culture itself did not disappear, the nation no longer posed a threat to the West. Alexander was able to exact the revenge that was the founding mission of the League of Corinth.

Alexandria was another of Alexander's major contributions to the world. Founded in 332 B.C.E., Alexandria not only became a massive naval base but also became a center for learning. The Alexandrian

Library was the ultimate ancient library. Famous academics like Euclid, Archimedes, and Eratosthenes studied philosophy, mysticism, science, and geography there (Reimer & Mackie, 2019).

Thirdly, in many ways, Alexander's expeditions paved the way for the Roman Empire. The knowledge of Middle and Far Eastern geography and cultures gave the Romans a better understanding of a world they eventually conquered (The Editors of Encyclopædia Britannica, 2020a).

Finally, and most importantly, Alexander and his conquests were responsible for the spread of Greek culture. Alexander the Great came from Macedonia, but he was raised largely by Athenian tutors and scholars. When he conquered new territory, he didn't replace the political structures or customs of the region, but he encouraged the spread of Greek culture. Toward the end of his life, Alexander pursued a more Persian lifestyle to appease the foreigners he ruled, but the impact of his ideas continued to spread beyond his death (*Alexander's Empire*, 2023).

Alexander's reign sowed the seeds of the Hellenistic Age. Greek culture influenced all of the people Alexander encountered, from the matrilineal Meroitic kingdom in Nubia to the Egyptian and Indian peoples. The Greek language and coins became a necessity for trade from Greece to Persia and to India beyond. Alexander might be gone, but Hellenism was now fully underway (*Alexander the Great*, 2019).

The Dawn of the Hellenistic Era

With the passing of Alexander, a new era dawned on the Greek world. The world of trade, politics, and culture would be transformed, paving a path through upheaval to a new world order underneath the Romans. However, power still remained in the Middle East and beyond. India and China now made contact more regularly with the Greeks, Persians, and Egyptians. A common language, the Greek language, would shape economic and political policies for centuries to come.

Before he died, someone asked Alexander, "Who is your empire going to go to?"

Alexander replied, "To the strongest man."

The question then became: Who was the strongest man?

In the next chapter, we'll examine the Diadochi, or "successors," of Alexander the Great: Cassander, Ptolemy, Antigonus, and Seleucus. Beyond the Succession Wars lay the Hellenistic period, where the cultural and political legacies of Alexander took on new forms and spread even further.

Chapter 8: The Hellenistic Period

The sun dawns in the east, glinting on the dark waters of the Mediterranean Sea. Sandy beaches run up to the great walls of the port city of Alexandria, the jewel of the Hellenistic world. Close by, the Lighthouse of Alexandria rises on the nearby isle of Pharos as a monument to the city's grandeur, as well as a practical beacon for the ships coming into port.

Behind Alexandria's walls, streets follow the straight lines of a grid system in an organized layout. This is uncommon in other ancient Egyptian cities. Gorgeous edifices of theaters, public buildings, and temples line the bustling streets.

From the shadows of a great conqueror emerged an age of culture. The Hellenistic period lasted from 323 B.C.E. to 31 B.C.E. It set the stage for future advancements and political change.

The Successor Kingdoms

Alexander's death came as a shock. It was too sudden and too soon. People back in Greece refused to believe the news at first.

Alexander and Roxana's son was still just a baby. Alexander hadn't left a regent clearly in control. Whatever Alexander's choice, any decision, either in favor of his infant son or his friend, Perdiccas, was ignored.

Chaos plunged his fledgling empire into a struggle for power. Friends battled friends, and wives battled wives, allying themselves with different factions. Among the leaders of Alexander's empire, known as the Daidochi, or "successors," four major names vied for power: Cassander, Ptolemy, Antigonus, and Seleucus.

In the following years, Cassander hunted down and killed Olympias, Roxana, and Alexander's son, Alexander IV, who was around 12 years old at the time. Cassander was swiftly routed by Antigonus. This left three major figures to claim and fight for territory.

Over a period of 40 years, Seleucus, Ptolemy, and Antigonus stabilized their chosen regions. This ushered in a new era of cultural and economic advancement. While none of these men matched Alexander's charisma, intelligence, or military genius, their dynasties were secured until the arrival of the Romans (Mark, 2013).

The Seleucids

The Seleucid Empire (312–63 B.C.E.) was the largest territory left after Alexander's death. Claimed by Seleucus, it included a large portion of Mesopotamia, Anatolia, and northwestern India. After a two-year war and negotiations with King Chandragupta Maurya in the east, Seleucus looked back to the other successor kingdoms.

Seleucus contested territory with Antigonus, beating his old friend in 310 B.C.E. By 301 B.C.E., Seleucus controlled the largest portion of Alexander's old empire. He founded a new capital city, Antioch, on the Orontes River. His son helped him rule from the other capital city, Seleucia, in the east.

In 281 B.C.E., circumstances gave Seleucus the chance to take Anatolia from Lysimachus, another, less successful Daidochos. After defeating and killing Lysimachus, Seleucus was the last of the surviving Diadochi and the new ruler of Anatolia. Later that year, Seleucus was busy with preparations to invade Greece. He never achieved that dream, assassinated by Ptolemy Ceraunos, the oldest son of his friend Ptolemy, in a bid for control over Anatolia.

Out of the four men, Seleucus was able to not only hold the largest portion of land but also achieve what Alexander had dreamed of—a multicultural empire, where Western and Eastern culture fused. Underneath the Seleucid Dynasty, Seleucus and his heirs successfully encouraged cultural fusion, religious tolerance, organized governance, and lucrative trade (Mark, 2019).

The Ptolemies

The Ptolemaic Dynasty (305–30 B.C.E.) wasn't as big as the Seleucid Empire. Ptolemy, known for being "enterprising," claimed Egypt. A close friend and bodyguard of Alexander, Ptolemy realized that Alexander's son would never rule. He instantly went to Egypt.

Ptolemy believed Egypt was perfect since it was ideally positioned and rich in resources. The Egyptians didn't seem to mind. After all, Alexander had freed them from an oppressive Persian rule, had worshipped at their temples, had built a new temple to honor Isis, and had given them the freedom to worship their preferred faith and preserve their cultural traditions.

Like Alexander, Ptolemy continued to reign in a tolerant way. He focused on stabilizing the country. Although he found himself caught up in the Successor Wars, Ptolemy worked to revive Egypt, create a haven for Greek and Macedonian culture in Alexandria, and bring prosperity to his people.

When he died in 282 B.C.E., his successor Ptolemy II came to power. The start of Ptolemy II's reign was rough. He got caught up in a war with Lysimachus and Antiochus I, among other conflicts.

However, at home, Ptolemy II continued his father's program. He created trading posts along the coast of the Red Sea, finished the lighthouse, Pharos, made the Alexandrian Library even larger, and improved the famous museum located there. Both Ptolemy I and his son, although Macedonian by blood, were considered the last two great Pharaohs of Egypt (Wasson, 2016).

The Antigonids

The Antigonid Dynasty (306–168 B.C.E.) did not last as long as the others. The homeland of Macedonia was a hotly contested territory. Back in 333 B.C.E., Alexander had put Antigonus I in charge of Phrygia as a satrap. He received the governorship of other areas upon Alexander's death. However, with allies at his back, Antigonus was able to take control of Macedonia.

Antigonus' ambitions to rebuild Alexander's empire did not go unnoticed. His old allies, such as Ptolemy, switched sides in an effort to stop Antigonus from taking over. The war didn't last long. By 312 B.C.E., Antigonus recognized that peace was necessary. Excepting Seleucus, Antigonus created treaties with the rest of his opponents.

However, this peace ended as ambitions between the Diadochi came to the surface yet again. Antigonus and his son Demetrius went to war, once again pursuing old enemies. In 301 B.C.E., the armies of Lysimachus and Seleucus attacked Antigonus at the Battle of Ipsus. The 80-year-old king was killed, leaving Demetrius in charge (Volkmann, 2019a).

Despite the death of Antigonus I, he left behind a strong legacy for his descendants. Not only had he expanded his territory, but he had also created new cities from united smaller communities, such as Teos and Lebedus. However, like the other successor kingdoms, the Antigonid Dynasty experienced its ups and downs under strong and weak rulers.

One of its strongest rulers, the grandson of Antigonus I, Antigonus II Gonatas, worked hard to stabilize the territory he claimed. A student of Zeno, the father of Stoicism, Antigonus II's views on governance and rulership were rather different from the other dynasties and empires. Antigonus II believed that rulers ought to serve the people and the law. Besides inviting Zeno to his court, Antigonus II also encouraged the arts and other academic pursuits (Volkmann, 2019b).

Greco-Bactrians and Indo-Greeks

While Alexander's reign as a king and emperor was cut short, the warrior-king was able to realize many of his imperial dreams. Thanks to his conquests, Alexander ensured that Greek culture would flourish and evolve in places far outside the Aegean. While he didn't forcefully impose much of his culture on his newly acquired territories, cross-pollination of ideas and cultural activity was bound to happen.

The Greco-Bactrian Kingdom, also known as "the land of a thousand cities," is a prime example of Alexander's effect on history. Despite its distance from Greece, Greeks had settled in the area before Alexander's conquests. Since then, the Greek colonies there had been subjugated by the Persians, as far back as the Greco-Persian Wars in the mid-400s B.C.E.

This kingdom gathered more power as the post-Alexandrian dynasties faltered. The Bactrian Kingdom gained independence around the 3rd century B.C.E. Its first king, Diodotus I Soter was a Bactrian-born Greek. Over time, the kingdom grew to include modern-day eastern Iran, Turkmenistan, Uzbekistan, Tajikistan, Afghanistan, and Pakistan.

Many of the cities in the Greco-Baktrian Kingdom, such as Ai-Khanoum, looked like other *poleis* in the Greek homeland. They had large urban centers complete with theaters, gymnasiums, gateways, mausoleums, and main streets. Surviving Greek-styled art, mosaics, and sculpture reveal aesthetics similar to what was produced in Greece. Scholars from Greece traveled to the largest urban centers of the Greco-Bactrian Kingdom, bringing with them philosophical writing, maxims, and even plays (Fernandes, 2022).

Around 190 B.C.E., another Greco-Bactrian king, Demetrius I, extended his borders southward into modern-day northwestern India. The Indo-Greek Kingdom that arose there became its own nation, spreading across parts of modern-day Pakistan and northern India. However, by 130 B.C.E., the Greco-Bactrian Kingdom was fragmented under invasions from the rising Parthians (Stamatios, 2023).

In the Indo-Greek Kingdom, the Greeks and Indians mixed freely. Over time, the Greeks, also known as Yonas, took on more Indian characteristics. The kingdom survived civil wars and invasions, outlasting the Greco-Bactrian Kingdom from which it derived by more than a century. It was eventually vanquished around 10 B.C.E. by Indo-Sakan invaders. By then, the Indo-Greek culture was far from its origins in Greece. But while their culture eventually faded, artifacts remain, pointing to a diverse and vibrant culture (Simonin, 2011).

Hellenistic Culture: Art, Science, and Philosophy

What does "Hellenistic" mean? Hellenism, or Hellenization, refers to the spread of Greek culture, particularly its language and people. Thanks to Alexander's conquests, Greeks were now living in Asia Minor, the Middle East, North Africa, and the Far East. While many fused with the native cultures, intermarrying and sharing traditions, the Greeks and their new neighbors began to rely on Greek ways of doing commerce, among other traditions.

Evolving Art and Culture

During the Hellenistic Period, the Greeks didn't just spread their ideas to other nations and peoples. Their art, architecture, and literature also began to shift and expand. New forms of art, music, and writing emerged in the two centuries after Alexander's death.

For example, architecture became more dramatic. The Corinthian aesthetic became incredibly popular. The Corinthian order was characterized by slender, fluted columns sitting on a base. The column's capital (the broad section at the top of columns or pillars) was shaped into stylized acanthus leaves or tendrils. It was very delicate and natural looking.

Another popular architectural element that emerged was the stoa, a covered walkway, usually with one side lined with columns. These walkways, or, porticos circled an open space or agora.

Hellenistic sculpture advanced even further. One fine example is the Gigantomachy, which shows the Titans and the Olympian gods fighting each other. Other sculptures, like the Dying Gaul, show how sculpture changed dramatically during this period. In one rendition of the Dying Gaul type, a Gallic chief holds his wife, whom he just killed to avoid slavery. He has taken his knife to himself, committing suicide right after.

Nike of Samothrace. Venus de Milo. The Barberini Faun. All of these are a testament to the lasting power of Greek art. Instead of having human bodies standing stiffly (in stark contrast to Minoan, Mycenaean, Archaic, and even Classical statuary) the figures from the Hellenistic period are emotive and natural-looking. The clothing details, poses, and even textured skin created a powerful sense of dynamism. Since these sculptures were so dramatic, the art during this period became the primary inspiration for European art for centuries to come (Buis, 2023).

The Role of Alexandria

Alexander founded quite a few cities (most named Alexandria), but the greatest city he created was undoubtedly Alexandria in Egypt. For more than 2,000 years, Alexandria remained the largest and most important city in Egypt. On the shores of the Mediterranean Sea, this city was an important port, where navies and traders alike could gather.

Scholars from all walks of life gathered there, from Greek philosophers to Eastern mystics and Jewish leaders. The Alexandrian Library was its main draw. It was said to have around 500,000 books, an astronomical number in days before the printing press. As a result, philosophers, scientists, writers, mathematicians, and religious men visited Alexandria to study and write. In Alexandria, famous thinkers like Archimedes and Euclid formulated philosophical and mathematical theories.

When Alexander died, his body was eventually laid to rest in Alexandria. Ptolemy, taking control of Egypt, nurtured the city. He continued work on its infrastructure, organizing it into a grid system, ensuring that the port was designed for maximum efficiency, and building beautiful public spaces for its citizens. Its public buildings, theaters, and temples fused Greek and Egyptian aesthetics in glorious harmony. In many ways, Alexandria represented the fruition of the Hellenistic endeavor (Mason, 2023).

Emergence of Schools of Thought

During Philip's exploits, Alexander the Great's conquests, and the Successor Wars, the Greek field of philosophy continued to develop. Plato's Academy and Aristotle's Lyceum continued the work of developing concepts around general philosophy as well as virtues, ethics, and other ways to "live a good life." During the Hellenistic period, however, other schools of thought began to emerge: Epicureanism, Cynicism, and Stoicism.

Epicurus (341–271 B.C.E.) pursued an extreme materialist philosophy. He believed everything, including the soul, was made of atoms. He also believed that these atoms were not designed to follow predetermined paths, nor that they were passive.

Therefore, he posited, there was an element of chance in the universe.

His scientific beliefs about physics and chance led him to believe that humans had free will and the right to pursue a good life. Good living, he said, could be achieved by pursuing pleasure (*hedone*). However, it was limited by an equal respect for reason, tranquility, and delayed gratification.

According to Epicurus, pain, if the end result would bring more pleasure, shouldn't be avoided. Unfortunately, many people came to believe that Epicureans were allowed to just do whatever they wanted. As a result, "Epicurean" became the byword for hedonism (a word that derives from *hedone*), although Epicurus's initial hedonism was, in fact, nuanced and limited (Graham, 2023).

Antisthenes (c. 445–366 B.C.E.) and, more famously, Diogenes of Sinope (c. 404–323 B.C.E.) espoused the philosophy of Cynicism. This school of thought was never formalized. This was because Cynics didn't believe that formalities, social conventions, or cultural expectations were healthy.

Pushing some of Socrates' ideas to the extreme, Diogenes believed that you didn't need a lot to be happy. Diogenes, among other cynics, pursued a minimalist life that was close to nature and natural self-expression. Diogenes didn't wear great clothing or eat a lot. He spent much of his time mocking the everyday life and choices of his fellow Greeks.

This got Cynics into trouble. Diogenes' pursuit of contentment in all circumstances was embraced by other Cynics. However, the Cynics would never become a fully formed school because of its inherently individualistic and fragmented nature (Graham, 2023).

Zeno of Citium (c. 334–242 B.C.E.) founded the first Stoic school. Focusing on science, logic, and ethics as a way to make sense of the world, the Stoics followed the same path as the Cynics in some ways. Like the Cynics, they recommended a life that is simpler and closer to nature. Furthermore, while they were materialists; they did not see matter as active, and they believed that God (*logos*) energizes matter as an organizing principle (Graham, 2023).

Since the universe was deterministic with limited free will, the Stoics believed that the path to a good life involved contemplation and acceptance. They encouraged their disciples to recognize when to exercise free will and when to accept things they couldn't change. The four basic tenets of Stoicism include courage (the ability to act in the face of fear), temperance (self-control), justice (how to relate well to people), and wisdom (the use of philosophy to know how to act in good or bad situations) (Lake, 2022).

Like Epicureanism, Stoicism became misunderstood over time. Many people today link it to emotional neglect or repression. This is far from what Zeno and other Stoics originally intended-a way to therapeutically gain perspective and spark self-empowerment.

Hypatia and the Hellenistic Tradition

One of the best examples of the lasting influence of the Hellenistic flowering of Greek culture is the life and work of Hypatia. Born in Alexandria around the year 355 C.E., about 300 years after the end of the Hellenistic period, Hypatia was the daughter of a well-known astronomer and mathematician. After spending years in his tutelage, Hypatia continued his work after he died, also tackling projects that interested her.

Hypatia became known for her work in the fields of mathematics, philosophy, and astronomy. The young woman preserved Greek knowledge during a period when the political landscape was in the midst of upheaval. She wrote commentaries on geometry, numbers, and astronomical tables, and synthesized information from numerous sources to preserve knowledge that might otherwise have been lost. At the same time, Hypatia lectured on philosophy to a loyal audience.

While not many of her philosophical works have remained, it appears that Hypatia was a Neoplatonist: one of a series of thinkers who borrowed heavily from Plato and later Hellenistic philosophers. Many great religious figures were influenced by Neoplatonic thought, including St. Augustine, Avicenna, and Maimonides. Due to Hypatia's philosophy and desire to pursue the One, the underlying reality Plato had spoken of, Hypatia embraced a life of celibacy.

Unfortunately, when the moderate governance of Alexandria collapsed in 414-415 C.E., the Roman prefect and ally of Hypatia, Orestes, struggled to keep control. In support of the newly appointed Cyril, patriarch of Alexandria, Christian cultists, most likely fanatical Nitrian monks or followers of a populist preacher named Peter, took to the streets to cleanse the city.

Hypatia was brutally murdered by one such gang. There is no consensus among scholars whether she died because of her paganism, her scholarship, or her political connection to Orestes. Nevertheless, Hypatia later became an example of early feminist scholarship as well as martyred academics in general. Whatever the case, Hypatia was an influential scholar in the Hellenistic tradition dedicated to learning and knowledge (Deakin, 2019).

New Powers Rising: Rome and Parthia

Inevitably, the power of the Ptolemaic Dynasty, the Antigonid Dynasty, and the Seleucid Empire all dwindled. Faced with new threats from the Parthians and the Romans, these kingdoms had to make a decision. Would they ally themselves with the new world powers, or would they fight?

Of the three, the Antigonid Dynasty ended first, in 168 B.C.E. Macedonia was Rome's first target in the east. After conflict and uneasy truces, Perseus, the last king of the Antigonid Dynasty, was defeated by the Romans at the Battle of Pydna in 168 B.C.E. (The Editors of the Encyclopaedia Britannica, 2021).

The Seleucid Empire proved too difficult to unite for many of Seleucus' descendants. Headed by kings more concerned with enjoying life and looking good, the Empire proved lethargic while invaders annexed territory satraps rebelled. Like many Seleucid kings after the brief resurgence under Antiochus III (241-187 B.C.E.), the last king, Philip II, lost his territory to the Parthians. The vision of a Greek empire in the east was gone after 56 B.C.E.

The Ptolemaic Dynasty didn't fare much better. Increasingly, the Ptolemaic monarchs struggled with civil war, family feuding, and the threat of Rome. When Rome began to extend eastwards, the Ptolemaic Dynasty became uneasy puppets of the new imperial power from the west. The last Ptolemaic pharaoh of Egypt was the infamous and tragic Cleopatra VII (Wasson, 2016). She died in 30 B.C.E., caught up on the losing side of Rome's civil war.

Parthians: The Eastern Buffer

One of the two powers that confronted the Seleucid, Ptolemaic, and Antigonid dynasties was the Parthian Empire (247 B.C.E.–224 C.E.), which lasted around 500 years. The Empire stretched from the Mediterranean Sea, including the old territory of Persia, all the way to India in the east. Initially, Parthia was part of the Seleucid Empire as one of the satrapies. The nomadic Parni tribe, however, managed to control the area, and by 247 B.C.E., had gained quite a bit of territory by the Caspian Sea. After defeating Antiochus VII of the Seleucid Dynasty at the Battle of Ecbatana in 129 B.C.E., they were able to expand even more.

Rome, however, had different plans. The two clashed over Armenia. The Parthians won, enlarging their territory. For a while, it seemed like the Parthians would be able to hold their own. This was due to their very unique fighting strategies. They used incredibly mobile fighting units that could pretend to retreat and then turn quickly or do hit-and-run strikes on the enemy. Using horse archers, the Parthians learned how to twist in the saddle and shoot from the back of a horse. This way, they could retreat and attack at the same time. This style of warfare frustrated many other opponents; and, to this day, a verbal zinger sent to an opponent to get the last word in is called a "Parthian Shot."

At the Battle of Carrhae in 53 B.C.E., the Parthians soundly defeated the Romans, taking the Roman standards captive. This was a severe blow to Roman morale. Crassus, who led the Roman army, was an ambitious politician and general who wanted the resources and wealth of the East for himself.

After facing Surena and his army on a tributary of the Euphrates River near the city of Carrhae, Crassus overestimated his power. Surena had successfully hidden the true size of his army behind hides, cloaks, and a wide frontline. Upon the death of his son during an unsuccessful counterattack, Crassus collapsed.

His army of 43,000 was decimated in a day. Their retreat to Carrhae ended in refusals to accept a ceasefire. Crassus ended up dead, and Rome reeled from the loss of a powerful political leader and a large army (Hudson, 2019).

In the meantime, Parthia continued to enjoy the fruits of their territorial consolidation. By taking care of the roads and governmental infrastructure that they took from the Seleucid Empire, the Parthians were able to pick up old alliances and encourage the continuation of trade. They were also able to establish control over the Silk Road, allowing them to capitalize on the lucrative trade between China and the Mediterranean (Smith, 2019). The Parthians wouldn't survive forever, but for now, they managed to hold their own. It was only a matter of time before Rome returned.

Rome: Republic to Empire

Ultimately it was the second power, the Romans, that ended the three dynasties. The early days of the Roman Republic were rocky. As Greece reached the height of the Classical Period in the mid-5th century B.C.E., Rome was struggling with its Latin, Etruscan, and other Italic neighbors for control of central Italy. However, it slowly became dominant, absorbing many of the surrounding peoples and dealing with the consequent social and economic fallout through the 4th and early 3rd centuries B.C.E. Finally, after its first two major wars with Carthage (264-201 B.C.E.), Rome became a true imperial power.

Administering provinces outside Italy strained the political apparatus of a city-state, and the Roman Republic struggled to accommodate the growing influence of its generals and magistrates, leading to an increase in political violence after 133 B.C.E. A century of intermittent civil war followed.

However, Roman civil strife did not derail its expansion, and the internally dysfunctional Republic was an externally unstoppable military power that encroached on the Successor Kingdoms more and more.

The Fall of Macedon and the Seleucid Empire

A series of 4 Macedonian Wars (214-148 B.C.E.) thoroughly dismantled the Antigonid kingdom of Macedon, culminating in the complete sack of Corinth in 146 B.C.E., the same year Rome razed Carthage. Rome had conquered mainland Greece. Many Greek cities in western Anatolia followed when the Hellenistic King Attalus III of Pergamum left his kingdom to the Roman Republic in his will in 133 B.C.E. The territory became the Roman province of Asia.

The Greek independent spirit flared up again in 88 B.C.E., when another Hellenistic king, Mithridates VI of Pontus, declared war on Rome and invaded Asia. To expel Rome's influence from the East permanently, Mithridates massacred 100,000 Roman citizens in Anatolia, an episode now called the "Asiatic Vespers." He sent forces into Greece, and many *poleis* revolted against Roman control. Rome declared war.

The Mithridatic Wars raged until 63 B.C.E. Mithridates proved to be one of the Roman Republic's great antagonists, holding his own both politically and on the battlefield. Nevertheless, the Hellenistic phalanx could not stand toe-to-toe with the Roman legion. The Roman politician and general Gnaeus Pompeius Magnus (Pompey the Great) formally incorporated Anatolia and the last remaining dreg of the Seleucid Empire into the Roman provinces of Asia, Bithynia and Pontus, Cilicia, and Syria. Rome ruled the Near East, and 2 of the great Hellenistic powers were no more.

The End of the Republic and the Fall of Ptolemaic Egypt

In 60 B.C.E., Pompey formed a political alliance with Gaius Julius Caesar and Marcus Licinius Crassus (who would later die at Carrhae fighting the Parthians). Despite Rome's republican structure, the three men forced through the measures they preferred over the next decade. After Crassus was killed at the Battle of Carrhae, Pompey and Caesar remained in power, gaining influence—which eventually drew them into direct conflict with each other (Appleton, 2022).

Crossing from Gaul (modern France) into Italy over the Rubicon River in 49 B.C.E., Caesar returned to Rome at the head of his army. It was an act of war, but Pompey fled. Caesar pursued him, beat him at the Battle of Pharsalus in 48 B.C.E., and forced him to again flee to Ptolemaic Egypt. Pompey, however, was killed by the Egyptians, who believed the gods favored Caesar. Julius Caesar was furious at the murder of his one-time friend.

At this point, Caesar was approached by the infamous Cleopatra VII. After deposing (and effectively killing) the teenage Ptolemy XIII, Caesar aligned himself with her. Cleopatra, born of the Ptolemaic line, understood Egypt. She was the only Ptolemaic ruler to learn how to read and write Egyptian. She was also more in touch with Egyptian culture even though she descended from a long line of Macedonian Greeks.

Recognizing that she needed Caesar's support to keep her throne, Cleopatra practiced careful diplomacy, showing herself to be one of the most formidable politicians of her era. Caesar accepted Cleopatra's support, giving her the regency of Egypt, which she was to co-rule with her younger brother, Ptolemy XIV. Caesar and Cleopatra maintained a passionate love affair until his assassination, producing a son, whom she named Caesarion.

Caesar returned victoriously to Rome in 46 B.C.E. Two years later, he was assassinated on the Ides of March (March 15th). Now Rome was beset by another power struggle between the most influential men left in Caesar's wake: Brutus, Cassius, Antony, and Octavian. Brutus and Cassius were forced to face Octavian and Antony, who temporarily teamed up to beat them at the Battle of Philippi in 42 B.C.E.

Mark Antony then joined Cleopatra in Egypt. At first, Antony harbored ambitious plans, hoping to invade Parthia. His expeditions only granted him temporary ownership of Armenia. Antony's triumphant return to Alexandria coincided with the announcement that Cleopatra's son, Caesarion, was in fact Julius Caesar's son, and therefore heir to Roman rule. Ptolemy XIV, with whom she shared rulership over Egypt, died, likely assassinated by Antony and Cleopatra.

Octavian, the nephew and adopted son of Julius Caesar, recognized the two as a threat. In a bid to consolidate his position, he challenged Antony and Cleopatra's forces at the Battle of Actium in 31 B.C.E. Octavian won, forcing the two to retreat to Alexandria and fight a rearguard defense (Tyldesley, 2019).

Ultimately, the love of Antony and Cleopatra was their one weakness. Hearing fake news of Cleopatra's death, Antony fell on his sword. He was taken to Cleopatra, where he died in her arms. Although Antony begged her to make peace with Octavian, Cleopatra committed suicide right after, allowing herself to be bitten by a poisonous snake. After killing Cleopatra's 17-year-old son, Caesarion, Octavian was now in control. The Roman Republic was dead, and the Hellenistic Period was over (Mark, 2011).

The Decline of the Hellenistic Period

The dissolution of Hellenistic political power was largely due to the fact that, as Rome conquered new territory, its language, culture, and political organization dominated the regions. Of course, Alexandria and the other Hellenistic cities were not entirely destroyed. Many retained their Greek influences and language. Rome, for example, encouraged hybrid cultures, as long as the people were loyal to the Roman emperor.

In fact, Romans admired Greek culture. They tried to connect themselves to some of the most famous Greek stories. The Aeneid is an example of this tendency, placing a Roman ancestor at the Battle of Troy as a way to culturally validate their authority.

Greece and most of its colonies and kingdoms were now vassal states of Rome. But Greek culture persisted (and persists), impacting nearly every aspect of Roman life. It raised the Roman citizens to new heights of artistic, musical, and philosophical appreciation (Hoekstra, 2021).

Far to the east, the Sassanid Persians (224-651 C.E.) also kept remnants of the Hellenistic influence with their own art, writings, and academic pursuits. The Sassanid rulers were tolerant, allowing multiple faiths to flourish, although they mainly supported Zoroastrianism. Khosrow I (531-579 C.E.) was particularly famous for supporting the Academy of Gundeshapur, where Iranian literature and religious texts, Greek philosophical texts, and Indian writings were gathered. Here, they translated many of these texts into several languages, which were shared with Europeans centuries later (Cervantes, 2013).

Foundation Not Forgotten

As the sun set on the Hellenistic period and the dawn of Roman dominance began, the indelible imprints of Greek thought, art, and governance continued to resonate throughout history. Although the reins of power now lay in different hands, their stories, art, advancements, and philosophy continued to shape the minds of Roman youths and future politicians. The tales of bravery, the questions of existence, the beauty of sculptures, and the rhythm of Greek dramas were not just tales of an era gone by; they were the foundations for many civilizations to come.

Conclusion

King Minos. Achilles. Homer. Solon. Leonidas. Pericles. Lysander. Socrates. Plato. Aristotle. Alexander.
Cleopatra. Hypatia. The list could continue, did continue, for ages. These are just a few of the great men
and women who directed the dramatic and epic history of ancient Greece. Their tales are filled with
dangerous, heartbreaking, and shocking events.
Their dreams and desires cost lives, expanded territory, and transformed the world.

Yet, there was another world in ancient Greece—
the scholars, the creatives, and the humble workers.
They tirelessly toiled to produce and consolidate the
knowledge they had gathered, perpetuating it for future generations. The artists, musicians, and writers
inspired each other, other countries, and many peoples throughout the centuries. Even more
importantly, it was on the backs of the diligent laborers, artisans, and farmers of Greece that the enduring
edifice of the Western tradition arose.

The Legacy of Greece

From their combined power, Greeks entrusted to
the future a glorious heritage. Their legacy will always
be remembered. For, thanks to Greece, art, architecture, academia, and politics will never be the same.

As we discovered, Greek art affected the entire ancient world. Their exported pottery, sculptures, jewelry, paintings, mosaics, clothes, and musical instruments influenced their neighbors. Furthermore, the art and music of Greece were perpetuated by their Roman successors. Through that Latin lineage, the cities of Venice, Florence, Paris, and even London were beautified with art and sculpture reminiscent of Greek aesthetics.

Greek architecture can also be seen across Europe and around the world. The Greek styles of Corinthian, Ionian, and Doric columns and capitals spread throughout the ancient world and are still used in modern times. Their monuments and public building designs were shared, inspiring future architects to attempt their own forms of beauty.

Academia was heavily impacted by Greek scholars. Math, science, medicine, philosophy, and history all exist on a Greek foundation. Thanks to Socrates, Aristotle, Plato, and many other Greek thinkers, ideas on how to learn, how to use logic, and how to define and classify the basis of the modern scientific method.

The philosophies they shared impacted secular and religious thought through the medieval era and even beyond, to modern thinkers. Furthermore, facts that we take for granted today—the heliocentric solar system, planetary movement, the Golden Ratio, and Pythagoras' theorem—were all formalized by the

Greeks. The Hippocratic Oath was the first time medicine and ethics combined to make a vow "to do no
harm."

Besides all that, Greek people and scholars also
impacted the literature and linguistics of many cultures beyond their own. Thanks to the Greeks, the
earliest Phoenician script evolved into what we know
as Classical Greek today. Coopted and further
evolved by the Romans, the more phonetic alphabet
ended up becoming an important piece of the English
and other European languages.

In the literary world, Greece inspired future writers with their own epic tales of Troy and Odysseus.
Ancient Greek playwrights formalized play structures, genres, and literary concepts, like irony; any
word ending in "onomy" or "ology" is rooted in the
Greek language. Other words like stadium, gymna-
sium, drama, and democracy originate from their
culture, as well.

History as Their Story

We owe a lot to the Greeks. When we read their
histories, it is important to remember that these people once lived as we did, with their own dreams,
ambitions, strengths, and flaws. Seen in this light, it
might become easier for you to recognize the inher-
ent drama of Greek history. Their stories, adventures,
and tragedies are ready and waiting for us to explore.

As the echoes of Ancient Greece resonate within
these pages, remember that the past holds treasures

that illuminate the paths of the future. If the tales, art, and philosophy within this volume stirred your spirit, share your insights and reviews. Recommend this book to friends, family, and anyone with a thirst for knowledge. The legacy of Greece is not just in its past, but in how its tales inspire the present.

Every era might have an end, but its stories, lessons, and inspirations endure. Dive deeper, discuss more, and let the spirit of inquiry guide your journey through history and life.

Note to the Reader

Sharing sincere feedback is the best way to support (and improve) the work of independent publishers. If you enjoyed and found value in this book, please leave a review and invite others to learn about and reflect upon our common past to build a promising future.

References

Achievements. (n.d.). Foundation of the Hellenic World.
http://www.fhw.gr/chronos/02/mainland/en/mg/achievements/index.html#:~:text=The%20Mycenaeans%20adopted%20the%20numeration

Alexander the Great. (2017). Khan Academy.
https://www.khanacademy.org/humanities/world-history/ancient-medieval/alexander-the-great/a/alexander-the-great

Alexander the Great. (2019). Ushistory.
https://www.ushistory.org/civ/5g.asp

Alexander's empire. (2023). Lumen Learning.
https://courses.lumenlearning.com/atd-herkimer-westerncivilization/chapter/alexanders-empire/

Alphabet (Early Greek). (2007, December 13). Joukowsky Institute for Archaeology.
https://www.brown.edu/Departments/Joukowsky_Institute/courses/greekpast/4739.html#:~:text=The%20early%20Greek%20alphabet%20was

Ambury, J. M. (2022). *Socrates.* Internet Encyclopedia of Philosophy.
https://iep.utm.edu/socrates/

Ancient Corinth. (2023). CyArk.
https://www.cyark.org/projects/ancient-corinth/in-

depth#:~:text=The%20Greek%20city%20of
%20Corinth

*Ancient DNA reveals origins of the Minoans
and Mycenaeans.* (n.d.). Max-Planck-Ge-
sellschaft. Retrieved August 31, 2023, from
https://www.mpg.de/11419864/origins-of-
minoans-and-mycenae-
ans#:~:text=The%20Mycenaean%20civiliza
tion%20

Ancient Greece. (n.d.). *Discovery Techbook.*
https://www.lee.k12.nc.us/cms/lib03/NC01
001912/Centricity/Domain/1464/An-
cient%20Greece%20geography%20mod.pdf

Ancient Greece geography: Landscape & map.
(2023). Study.com.
https://study.com/learn/lesson/anicent-
greece-geography-land-
scape.html#:~:text=Many%20of%20the%2
0Greek%20city

Ancient Greece: Impact of geography. (n.d.).
East Ramapo Central School District.
https://www.ercsd.org/site/han-
dlers/filedownload.ashx?moduleinstanceid
=195&dataid=2330&FileName=03-022---
Ancient-Greece--Impact-of-Geography-
handout.pdf

Ancient Greek farming lesson for kids. (2022).
Study.com. https://study.com/acad-
emy/lesson/ancient-greek-farming-lesson-
for-kids.html#:~:text=Wheat%2C%20bar-
ley%2C%20olives%2C%20and

Ancient wisdom: 21 famous Aristotle quotes.
(2023). DSF Antique Jewelry.

https://dsfantiquejewelry.com/blogs/inter-esting-facts/ancient-wisdom-21-famous-aristotle-quotes

Ansari, A. (2012, July 14). Alexander the not so great: History through Persian eyes. *BBC News.* https://www.bbc.com/news/maga-zine-18803290

Appleton, S. (2022, September 28). *Rome's transition from republic to empire.* National Geographic Society. https://education.nationalgeo-graphic.org/resource/romes-transition-republic-empire/

Archaeological site of Troy. (1998, December 2). UNESCO World Heritage Centre. https://whc.unesco.org/en/list/849/

Archaic Greece. (n.d.). Lumen Learning. https://courses.lumenlearning.com/atd-herkimer-westerncivilization/chapter/ar-chaic-greece/

Armstead, K. (2023). *Peloponnesian War: Causes & results.* Study.com. https://study.com/learn/lesson/peloponne-sian-war-causes-re-sults.html#:~:text=What%20were%20the%20three%20main

Athens vs Sparta - difference and comparison. (2019). Diffen. https://www.diffen.com/dif-ference/Athens_vs_Sparta

Bencze, A. (2014). *Art and craft in Archaic Sparta.* The Met's Heilbrunn Timeline of Art History. https://www.met-museum.org/toah/hd/spar/hd_spar.htm#:

~:text=In%20fact%2C%20in%20the%20sev
enth

Bennett, A. (2020, December 5). *10 reasons the ancient city of Alexandria was an intellectual powerhouse*. TheCollector. https://www.thecollector.com/ancient-city-alexandria-intellectual-powerhouse/

Betancourt, P. P. (1969). *The age of Homer: An exhibition of geometric and orientalizing Greek art*. Expedition Magazine. https://www.penn.museum/sites/expedition/the-age-of-homer/#:~:text=Herodotus%20suggested%20that%20he%20lived

Bileta, V. (2023, February 28). *4 battles from Alexander the Great's legendary Persian campaign*. TheCollector. https://www.thecollector.com/alexander-greatest-battles/

Blakeley, S. (2022a). *Plato's Theory of Forms*. Study.com. https://study.com/learn/lesson/plato-theory-forms-realm-physical.html#:~:text=Plato

Blakeley, S. (2022b). *The Iliad & The Odyssey by Homer*. Study.com. https://study.com/learn/lesson/iliad-odyssey-homer-summary-characters.html

Bliss, R. (2022). *The Greco-Persian Wars: Causes & results*. Study.com. https://study.com/learn/lesson/greco-persian-wars-results-significance.html

Bloks, M. (2015, July 22). *The seven wives of Philip II of Macedon*. History of Royal

Women. https://www.historyofroyal-women.com/the-royal-women/the-seven-wives-of-philip-ii-of-macedon/

Bloxham, J. (2016, April 12). *Nicias*. World History Encyclopedia. https://www.worldhistory.org/Nicias/

Boeree, C. G. (2000). *Epicureans and Stoics*. Shippensburg University. https://web-space.ship.edu/cgboer/latergreeks.html

Brinkhof, T. (2022, March 1). *Socratic problem: How Plato and other Greek writers invented Socrates*. Big Think. https://bigthink.com/the-past/socratic-problem-plato-socrates/

Brown, T. (2022, September 21). *The lasting legacy of ancient Greek leaders and philosophers*. National Geographic Society. https://education.nationalgeo-graphic.org/resource/lasting-legacy-ancient-greek-leaders-and-philosophers/

Bucephalus: the true story of Alexander the Great's legendary horse. (2023). History Skills. https://www.historyskills.com/class-room/ancient-history/bucephalus/#:~:text=Bucepha-lus%20accompanied%20Alexander%20on%20many

Buis, A. (n.d.). *Mycenaean art*. British Columbia/Yukon Open Authoring Platform. https://pressbooks.bccampus.ca/cavestoca-thedrals/chapter/738/

Buis, A. (2023). Hellenistic Period. *PressBooks*. https://pressbooks.bccampus.ca/cavestoca-thedrals/chapter/hellenistic/

Carr, K. (2017a, July 7). *Ancient Corinth - Myce-naean and Archaic*. Quatr.us Study Guides. https://quatr.us/greeks/ancient-corinth-mycenaean-ar-chaic.htm#:~:text=In%20the%20early%20Archaic%20period

Carr, K. (2017b, July 7). *Corinth, Greece in the Classical period*. Quatr.us Study Guides. https://quatr.us/greeks/corinth-classical-period.htm

Cartwright, M. (2009, September 2). *Corinth*. World History Encyclopedia. https://www.worldhistory.org/corinth/

Cartwright, M. (2013a, February 8). *Alcibiades*. World History Encyclopedia. https://www.worldhistory.org/Alcibiades/

Cartwright, M. (2013b, April 16). *Battle of Ther-mopylae*. World History Encyclopedia. https://www.worldhistory.org/thermopy-lae/

Cartwright, M. (2013c, May 5). *Battle of Sala-mis*. World History Encyclopedia. https://www.worldhistory.org/Bat-tle_of_Salamis/

Cartwright, M. (2013d, May 11). *Battle of Pla-taea*. World History Encyclopedia. https://www.worldhistory.org/Plataea/

Cartwright, M. (2013e, May 19). *Battle of Mara-thon*. World History Encyclopedia. https://www.worldhistory.org/marathon/

Cartwright, M. (2013f, June 6). *Polis*. World History Encyclopedia.

https://www.worldhistory.org/Po-
lis/#:~:text=The%20polis%20emerged%20
from%20the

Cartwright, M. (2016a, March 18). *Lysander.*
World History Encyclopedia.
https://www.worldhistory.org/Lysander/

Cartwright, M. (2016b, July 25). *Food & agriculture in Ancient Greece.* World History
Encyclopedia.
https://www.worldhistory.org/arti-
cle/113/food--agriculture-in-ancient-
greece/

Cartwright, M. (2018a, March 20). *Ancient
Greek government.* World History Encyclopedia.
https://www.worldhistory.org/Greek_Gov-
ernment/

Cartwright, M. (2018b, March 29). *Minoan Civilization.* World History Encyclopedia.
https://www.worldhistory.org/Mi-
noan_Civilization/

Cartwright, M. (2018c, May 7). *Greek colonization.* World History Encyclopedia.
https://www.worldhistory.org/Greek_Colo-
nization/

Cartwright, M. (2019, October 2). *Mycenaean
civilization.* World History Encyclopedia.
https://www.worldhistory.org/Myce-
naean_Civilization/

Cartwright, M. (2020, April 27). *The legacy of
the Ancient Greeks.* World History Encyclopedia.
https://www.worldhistory.org/collec-
tion/75/the-legacy-of-the-ancient-greeks/

Cason, T. S. (n.d.). *Cycladic, Minoan, and Mycenaean civilization*. Florida State College. https://fscj.pressbooks.pub/earlyhumanities/chapter/cycladic-and-minoan-civilization/#:~:text=The%20Minoan%20Civilization%20

Cervantes, A. C. (2013, May 17). *Sasanian Empire*. World History Encyclopedia. https://www.worldhistory.org/Sasanian_Empire/#:~:text=Although%20certainly%20still%20Hellenized%2C%20the

Chaliakopoulos, A. (2021, March 26). *Who were the Diadochi of Alexander The Great?* TheCollector. https://www.thecollector.com/who-were-the-diadochi-of-alexander-the-great/

Chrysopoulos, P. (2023a, January 2). *The first time all Greek people united together*. Greek Reporter. https://greekreporter.com/2023/04/02/league-corinth-greek-people-united/

Chrysopoulos, P. (2023b, January 28). *Decoding Linear A, the writing system of the ancient Minoans*. Greek Reporter. https://greekreporter.com/2023/01/28/decoding-linear-a-the-writing-system-of-the-ancient-minoans/

Classical Greek culture. (2018). Khan Academy. https://www.khanacademy.org/humanities/world-history/ancient-medieval/classical-greece/a/greek-culture

Claus, P. (2023, August 20). *Minoan language Linear A linked to Linear B in groundbreaking research*. Greek Reporter.

https://greekreporter.com/2023/08/20/mi
noan-language-linear-a-linear-b/

Cleopatra, Julius Caesar and Mark Antony: how the last pharaoh's love affairs shaped Ancient Egypt's fate. (2020, August 21). HistoryExtra. https://www.historyextra.com/period/ancient-egypt/cleopatralove-affairs-julius-caesar-mark-antony/

Cleopatra's relationships with Julius Caesar and Mark Antony. (2013, September 16). Scholaradvisor.com. https://www.scholaradvisor.com/essay-examples/cleopatrarelationships/

Cooper, J. M. (1998). *Socrates (469–399 BC).* Routledge Encyclopedia of Philosophy. https://www.rep.routledge.com/articles/biographical/socrates-469-399-bc/v-1

Coumoundouros, A. (n.d.). *Plato: The Republic.* Internet Encyclopedia of Philosophy. https://iep.utm.edu/republic/

Cox, T. (2017). *Ptolemy XIII Theos Philopator.* World History Encyclopedia. https://www.worldhistory.org/Ptolemy_XIII_Theos_Philopator/

Daniel, J. F., Broneer, O., & Grey, H. T. W. (1948). The Dorian Invasion: The setting. *American Journal of Archaeology, 52*(1), 107–110. https://doi.org/10.2307/500556

Davis, Dr. J. L. (2023, March 13). *Agriculture and settlement: Farm and field at Ancient Mycenaean Pylos.* Brewminate: A Bold Blend of News and Ideas. https://brewminate.com/agriculture-and-settlement-farm-and-field-at-ancient-mycenaean-py-los/

Deakin, M. (2019). Hypatia. *Encyclopædia Britannica.* https://www.britannica.com/biography/Hypatia

Decline of the Mycenaean Civilization (1250-1050 BCE). (2022, July 13). Climate in Arts and History. https://www.science.smith.edu/climatelit/decline-of-the-mycenaean-civilization-1250-1050-bce/

Dmitriev, S. (2011). The Macedonian peace of Philip II and Alexander the Great. *Oxford University Press EBooks*, 67–111. https://doi.org/10.1093/ac-prof:oso/9780195375183.003.0002

Dorian Invasion. (2023). Academic Accelrator. https://academic-accelerator.com/encyclopedia/dorian-invasion

Duignan, B. (2019a). Democritus. *Encyclopædia Britannica.* https://www.britannica.com/biography/Democritus

Duignan, B. (2019b). Plato and Aristotle: How do they differ? *Encyclopædia Britannica.* https://www.britannica.com/story/plato-and-aristotle-how-do-they-differ

Edwards, A. S. (2022, October 19). *Alexander's relationships: Facts and myths.* British Library. https://www.bl.uk/alexander-the-great/articles/alexanders-relationships-facts-and-myths

Effects of the Peloponnesian War. (2023). Lumen Learning. https://courses.lumenlearning.com/atd-herkimer-westerncivilization/chapter/ef-fects-of-the-peloponnesian-war/

Effects of the Persian Wars. (2023). Lumen Learning. https://courses.lumenlearn-ing.com/atd-herkimer-westerncivilization/chapter/effects-of-the-persian-wars/

Everything you ever wanted to know about the Rosetta Stone. (2017, July 14). The British Museum. https://www.britishmu-seum.org/blog/everything-you-ever-wanted-know-about-rosetta-stone#:~:text=The%20im-portance%20of%20this%20to

Example questions. (n.d.). Varsity Tutors. Re-trieved September 1, 2023, from https://www.varsitytutors.com/an-cient_history_greece-help/fall-of-mycenaean-civilization-and-the-greek-dark-ages

Feen, R. H. (1996). Keeping the balance: An-cient Greek philosophical concerns with population and environment. *Population and Environment, 17*(6), 447–458. https://www.jstor.org/stable/27503492

Fernandes, F. (2022, March 16). *The Bactrian Kingdom: Greeks at the extremities of the known world.* TheCollector. https://www.thecollector.com/bactria-greek-hellenistic-kingdom/

Gabriel, R. (2017, July 14). *Alexander the Great: Monster of Macedonia.* Historynet. https://www.historynet.com/alexander-the-monster/

Garrett, E. (2019). *The Socratic Method*. University of Chicago Law School. https://www.law.uchicago.edu/socratic-method

Geography of Ancient Greece. (n.d.). Students of History. https://www.studentsofhistory.com/geography-of-ancient-greece#:~:text=The%20Geography%20of%20Ancient%20Greece&text=The%20mountains%20of%20Ancient%20Greece

German, S. (2022). *Snake Goddess*. Khan Academy. https://www.khanacademy.org/humanities/ancient-art-civilizations/aegean-art1/minoan/a/snake-goddess

Gill, N. S. (2019a). *A timeline of the Peloponnesian War's major battles*. ThoughtCo. https://www.thoughtco.com/timeline-battles-treaties-peloponnesian-war-112444

Gill, N. S. (2019b). *Introduction to the Persian Wars*. ThoughtCo. https://www.thoughtco.com/introduction-to-the-greco-persian-wars-120245

Golden, J. (2012). *Chapter 16: Battle of Carrhae Romans versus the Parthians*. O'Reilly. https://www.oreilly.com/library/view/winning-the-battle/9780071791991/ch16.html#:~:text=The%20Battle%20of%20Carrhae%2C%20fought

Graham, J. N. (2023). *Ancient Greek philosophy*. Internet Encyclopedia of Philosophy.

https://iep.utm.edu/ancient-greek-philoso-phy/#H5

Greek Boston. (2017a, March 22). *Rise of the Mycenaean Civilization in Ancient Greece.* Greek Boston. https://www.greekboston.com/culture/an-cient-history/rise-mycenaean-civilization/

Greek Boston. (2017b, May 26). *About the Do-rian Invasion of Ancient Greece.* Greek Boston. https://www.greekboston.com/cul-ture/ancient-history/dorian-invasion/

Greek city-states. (2022, May 20). National Ge-ographic Society. https://education.nationalgeo-graphic.org/resource/greek-city-states/

Greek Ministry of Culture. (1999). *The archaeo-logical sites of Mycenae and Tiryns.* https://whc.unesco.org/uploads/nomina-tions/941.pdf

Griffith, G. T. (2019). Philip II . *Encyclopædia Britannica.* https://www.britan-nica.com/biography/Philip-II-king-of-Macedonia

Groarke, L. F. (n.d.). *Aristotle: Logic.* Internet Encyclopedia of Philosophy. https://iep.utm.edu/aristotle-logic/

Gulati, A. (n.d.). *Delian League.* Brown Univer-sity. https://www.brown.edu/Depart-ments/Joukowsky_Institute/courses/greek past/4773.html

Hall, E. (2021, May 27). *Cynics, Stoics, Epicure-ans.* Gresham College.

https://www.gresham.ac.uk/watch-now/cynics-stoics-epicureans

Hanselman, S. (2020, October 6). *Stoicism vs. Epicureanism*. Daily Stoic. https://dailystoic.com/stoicism-vs-epicureanism/

Haskett, D. R., Racine, V., & Yang, J. (2016, July 7). *Aristotle (384-322 BCE)*. The Embryo Project Encyclopedia. https://embryo.asu.edu/pages/aristotle-384-322-bce#:~:text=During%20Aristotle

Hatch, P. (n.d.). *Tholos tomb*. Brown University. https://www.brown.edu/Departments/Joukowsky_Institute/courses/greekpast/4904.html

Hays, J. (2018). *Seleucids and the division of Alexander's empire after his death*. Facts and Details. https://factsanddetails.com/world/cat56/sub366/entry-6412.html

Hellenistic Art: Hellenism in Classical Antiquity. (n.d.). Encyclopedia of Art and Classical Antiquities. http://www.visual-arts-cork.com/antiquity/hellenistic-art.htm

Hemingway, C. (2019a). *Ancient Greek colonization and trade and their influence on Greek art*. Metmuseum.org. https://www.metmuseum.org/toah/hd/angk/hd_angk.htm

Hemingway, C. (2019b). *Art of the Hellenistic Age and the Hellenistic Tradition*. The Metropolitan Museum of Art. https://www.metmuseum.org/toah/hd/haht/hd_haht.htm

Hemingway, S., & Hemingway, C. (2004). *The rise of Macedon and the conquests of Alexander the Great.* The Met's Heilbrunn Timeline of Art History. https://www.met-museum.org/toah/hd/alex/hd_alex.htm#:~:text=Phillip%20II%20instituted%20far%2Dreaching

Hirst, K. K. (2018). *Linear A: Early Cretan writing system.* ThoughtCo. https://www.thoughtco.com/linear-writing-system-of-the-minoans-171553

Historical context for Homer. (2019). Columbia College. https://www.college.columbia.edu/core/node/1744

History of Corinth. (2023). American School of Classical Studies at Athens. https://www.ascsa.edu.gr/excavations/ancient-corinth/about-the-excavations-1/history-timeline

History of Greece during Stone and Bronze Age. (n.d.). Greeka. Retrieved August 30, 2023, from https://www.greeka.com/greece-history/stone-bronze-age/#:~:text=The%20Stone%20Age

History of Greece: The Dark Ages. (2023). Ancient Greece. https://www.ancient-greece.org/history/dark-ages.html

History.com Editors. (2009a, November 9). *Cleopatra.* History. https://www.history.com/topics/ancient-egypt/cleopatra

History.com Editors. (2009b, November 9). *Pericles*. History. https://www.history.com/topics/ancient-greece/pericles

History.com Editors. (2009c, November 9). *Plato*. History. https://www.history.com/topics/ancient-greece/plato

History.com Editors. (2009d, November 9). *Socrates*. History. https://www.history.com/topics/ancient-greece/socrates

History.com Editors. (2018, August 21). *Stone Age*. History. https://www.history.com/topics/pre-history/stone-age

History.com Editors. (2019, August 22). *Aristotle*. History. https://www.history.com/topics/ancient-greece/aristotle

History.com Editors. (2023a, May 31). *Trojan War*. History. https://www.history.com/topics/ancient-greece/trojan-war#section_3

History.com Editors. (2023b, August 23). *Alexander the Great: Empire & death*. History. https://www.history.com/topics/ancient-greece/alexander-the-great#section_2

Hoekstra, K. (2021, November 5). *What brought about the end of the Hellenistic Period?* History Hit. https://www.historyhit.com/what-brought-about-the-end-of-the-hellenistic-period/

Hoffmann, H. (2000, January 12). *Western architecture - Mycenaean Greece*. Encyclopedia Britannica. https://www.britannica.com/art/Western-architecture/Mycenaean-Greece

Homer's World. (2011). Camel Unified School District. https://moodle.carmelunified.org/moodle/pluginfile.php/81883/mod_resource/content/1/Odyssey%20Textbook%20Homers%20World%202015-16.pdf

Hornblower, S. (2023, September 4). *Ancient Greek civilization.* Encyclopedia Britannica. https://www.britannica.com/place/ancient-Greece/Solon

Hudson, M. (2019, September 10). *Battle of Carrhae.* Encyclopedia Britannica. https://www.britannica.com/event/Battle-of-Carrhae

Hutton, S. (2023). *6.4 The spread of Hellenistic culture.* Teaching California. https://www.teachingcalifornia.org/inquiry-sets/6-4-the-spread-of-hellenistic-culture/#:~:text=First%20the%20Greeks%20

Hypatia. (2018). Famous Scientists. https://www.famousscientists.org/hypatia/

International Olympic Committee. (2021, April 27). *Welcome to the Ancient Olympic Games.* International Olympic Committee. https://olympics.com/ioc/ancient-olympic-games

Jarus, O. (2017, August 26). *Ancient Troy: The city and the legend.* Live Science. https://www.livescience.com/38191-ancient-troy.html

Jarus, O., & Gordon, J. (2017, August 31). *Alexander the Great: Facts, Biography & accomplishments.* Live Science.

https://www.livescience.com/39997-alex-
ander-the-great.html

Jones, E. J. (2018). Long Distance Trade and
the Parthian Empire: Reclaiming Parthian
Agency from an Orientalist Historiography.
Western Washington University.
https://cedar.wwu.edu/cgi/viewcon-
tent.cgi?article=1717&context=wwuet

Juma, N. (2019, July 22). *Socrates quotes on
life, wisdom & philosophy to inspire you.*
Everyday Power. https://everyday-
power.com/socrates-quotes/

Kampouris, N. (n.d.). *Odyssey: Homer's epic
poem is the world's most influential story.*
Greek Reporter.
https://greekreporter.com/2022/04/01/od-
yssey-homer-epic-poem-is-officially-the-
worlds-most-influential-story/

Kirk, G. S. (2023, July 7). *Homer.* Encyclopædia
Britannica. https://www.britannica.com/bi-
ography/Homer-Greek-poet#ref524682

Kivilo, M. (2010). *Early Greek poets' lives: The
shaping of the tradition.* Brill. https://li-
brary.oapen.org/bitstream/handle/20.500.
12657/29586/1000346.pdf

Klaeser, M. (2021, July 7). *Mycenaean society.*
World History Encyclopedia.
https://www.worldhistory.org/Myce-
naean_Society/#:~:text=Mycenaean%20so
ciety

Kordas, A., Lynch, R. J., Nelson, B., & Tatlock,
J. (2023, April 19). *3.1 Early Civilizations.*
Openstax. https://open-
stax.org/books/world-history-volume-

1/pages/3-1-early-civiliza-
tions#:~:text=The%20development%20of%
20early%20civilizations

Koutoupis, P. (2018, January 6). *In search of
the mythical King Minos, did the legendary
ruler really exist?* Ancient Origins: Reconstructing the Story of Humanity's Past.
https://www.ancient-origins.net/myths-
legends-europe/search-mythical-king-mi-
nos-did-legendary-ruler-really-exist-
009394

Koy, M. (2021, June 21). *The Greco-Bactrian
Kingdom.* The History Inquiry. https://me-
dium.com/the-history-inquiry/the-greco-
bactrian-kingdom-c4c37c87fc7

Kraut, R. (2004, March 20). *Plato.* Stanford Encyclopedia of Philosophy.
https://plato.stanford.edu/entries/plato/

Kraut, R. (2019). Socrates - Background of the
trial. *Encyclopædia Britannica.*
https://www.britannica.com/biog-
raphy/Socrates/Background-of-the-trial

Kraut, R. (2022, July 2). *Aristotle's ethics.* Stanford Encyclopedia of Philosophy.
https://plato.stanford.edu/entries/aristo-
tle-ethics/

Kruse, S. (2022, April 13). *The Socratic Method:
Fostering critical thinking.* The Institute for
Learning and Teaching. https://tilt.colos-
tate.edu/the-socratic-method/

Kuznetsov, I. (n.d.). *Greek ranges.* PeakVisor.
Retrieved August 30, 2023, from
https://peakvisor.com/range/greek-
ranges.html

Lake, T. (2021, October 26). *Socrates' philosophy: The ancient Greek philosopher and his legacy*. TheCollector. https://www.thecollector.com/socrates-philosophy-ancient-greek-philosopher-legacy/

Lake, T. (2022, December 20). *An in-depth understanding on the four virtues of Stoicism*. TheCollector. https://www.thecollector.com/four-cardinal-virtues-stoicism/

Largo, M. (2014, August 21). *Big, bad botany: Hemlock (Conium maculatum), the philosopher's choice*. Slate. https://slate.com/technology/2014/08/poisonous-plants-socrates-drank-hemlock-tea-as-his-preferred-mode-of-execution.html#:~:text=When%20his%20blood%20touched%20the

Leeming, D. A. (2023). *Who were the Cycladic and Minoan peoples and what was their history?* Papertrell. https://www.papertrell.com/apps/preview/The-Handy-Mythology-Answer-Book/Handy%20Answer%20book/Who-were-the-Cycladic-and-Minoan-peoples-and-what-was-their-/001137032/content/SC/52caff2e82fad14abfa5c2e0_default.html#:~:text=the%20Cycladic%20civilization%20had%20developed

Legacies of Ancient Greece. (2023). Study.com. https://study.com/learn/lesson/legacies-ancient-greece-contributions-influences-examples.html#:~:text=Euclid%20built%20off%20the%20number

Legacy of Ancient Greece. (2023). History for Kids.
https://www.historyforkids.net/legacy-of-an-
cient-greece.html

*Legacy of Ancient Greece: Art, government,
science & sports.* (2020). Study.com.
https://study.com/academy/lesson/legacy-
of-ancient-greece-art-government-science-
sports.html

Leonard, B., & Zimbler, S. (2016, April 13).
*Homer: inspiration and controversy [Info-
graphic].* OUPblog.
https://blog.oup.com/2016/04/homer-in-
spiration-and-
contro-
versy/#:~:text=Since%20then%2C%20scho
lars%20have%20used

Lewis, D. M. (2019). Pericles. In *Encyclopædia
Britannica.* https://www.britan-
nica.com/biography/Pericles-Athenian-
statesman

Linder, D. O. (2019). *The trial of Socrates.* Famous Trials. https://www.famous-
trials.com/socrates/833-home

Lloyd, J. (2016, December 22). *Periander.*
World History Encyclopedia.
https://www.worldhistory.org/Periander/

Logo-. (2017, April 19). Online Etymology Dic-
tionary.
https://www.etymonline.com/word/logo-
?ref=etymonline_crossreference

Lomas, K. (2014). Greek Colonialism, Archaeology of. In: Smith, C. (eds) Encyclopedia of
Global Archaeology. Springer, New York,

NY. https://doi.org/10.1007/978-1-4419-0465-2_1435

Lonsdale, D. M. (2011). The campaigns of Alexander the Great. *Oxford University Press EBooks*, 14–34. https://doi.org/10.1093/ac-prof:oso/9780199608638.003.0002

Mamakouka, I.-A. (2014, March 25). *10 of the most significant writers of Ancient Greece.* Greek Reporter . https://greekreporter.com/2014/03/25/10-of-the-most-significant-writers-of-ancient-greece/

Mann, M. J. (2013, October 30). *The bullet point Alexander: Philip II's wives.* The Second Achilles. https://thesecondachilles.com/2013/10/30/the-bullet-point-alexander-philip-iis-wives/

Mark, J. (2011, April 28). *Julius Caesar.* World History Encyclopedia. https://www.worldhistory.org/Julius_Caesar/

Mark, J. (2018, March 28). *Pericles.* World History Encyclopedia. https://www.worldhistory.org/pericles/

Mark, J. J. (2013, November 14). *Alexander the Great.* World History Encyclopedia. https://www.worldhistory.org/Alexander_the_Great/

Mark, J. J. (2015a, January 30). *Greek Dark Age.* World History Encyclopedia. https://www.worldhistory.org/Greek_Dark_Age/

Mark, J. J. (2015b, February 5). *Greek alphabet.*
World History Encyclopedia.
https://www.worldhistory.org/Greek_Alphabet/

Mark, J. J. (2019, October 22). *Seleucid Empire.*
World History Encyclopedia.
https://www.worldhistory.org/Seleucid_Empire/

Marlowe, C. (1604). *From Doctor Faustus
("Was this the face that launched a thousand ships?").* Representative Poetry
Online. https://rpo.library.utoronto.ca/content/doctor-faustus-was-face-launched-thousand-ships

Mason, M. K. (2023). *Alexandria and the Hellenistic World.* Www.moyak.com.
https://www.moyak.com/papers/ancient-alexandria.html

McLean, J. (n.d.). *Greek Dark Ages.* Lumen
Learning. https://courses.lumenlearning.com/atd-herkimer-westerncivilization/chapter/greek-dark-ages/

Meinwald, C. C. (2018). Plato. *Encyclopædia
Britannica.* https://www.britannica.com/biography/Plato

Messerly, J. (2014, October 17). *Summary of
Aristotle's theory of human nature.* Reason
and Meaning. https://reasonandmeaning.com/2014/10/17/theories-of-human-nature-chapter-9-aristotle-part-1/

Metaphysics summary. (n.d.). SuperSummary.
Retrieved September 9, 2023, from

https://www.supersummary.com/meta-physics/summary/

Meyer, I. (2022a, April 13). *Hellenistic Art – Ancient Greek multiculturalism.* Art in Context. https://artincontext.org/hellenistic-art/

Meyer, I. (2022b, May 6). *Archaic Greek art - an overview of the Greek Archaic period.* Art in Context. https://artincontext.org/ar-chaic-greek-art/

Movellán Luis, M. (2018, January 31). *Rise and fall of the mighty Minoans.* History. https://www.nationalgeographic.com/his-tory/history-magazine/article/Minoan_Crete

Muscato, C. (2019). *Pericles of Athens: Facts, achievements & death.* Study.com. https://study.com/academy/lesson/peri-cles-of-athens-facts-achievements-death.html

Mycenae architecture: Info & photos. (n.d.). Greeka. https://www.greeka.com/pelopon-nese/mycenae/architecture/#:~:text=One%20of%20the%20distinctive%20features

Mycenaean architecture: History, characteris-tics & influences. (2021, December 5). Study.com. https://study.com/acad-emy/lesson/mycenaean-architecture-history-characteristics-influences.html

Mycenaean civilization. (2023). Study.com. https://study.com/learn/lesson/myce-naean-civilization-social-structure.html#:~:text=The%20Mycenae-ans%20flourished%20c.

Mycenaean warrior vase, 12th century BCE. (n.d.). Brock University. https://brocku.ca/blogs/brock-odyssey-2017/2017/06/17/mycenaean-warrior-vase-12th-century-bce/#:~:text=Myce-naean%20Clay%20is%20well%20known

Myers, C., Caldwell, E. C., Taylor, A. J., Phelps, M., & Soccio, L. (2021, July 7). *8.3: Mycenaean.* Humanities LibreTexts. https://human.libretexts.org/Bookshelves/Art/Introduction_to_Art_History_I_(Myers)/08%3A_The_Ancient_Aegean/8.03%3A_Mycenaean

Nagy, G. (2017). *Homer, Odyssey.* Columbia. https://edblogs.columbia.edu/worldepics/project/homer-odyssey/

Nails, D. (2018). *Socrates.* Stanford Encyclopedia of Philosophy. https://plato.stanford.edu/entries/socrates/

Nair, S. S. (2017, March 2). *Philosopher Plato quotes on knowledge and learning.* YourStory. https://yourstory.com/2017/03/29-quotes-by-plato#:~:text=%E2%80%9CTruth%20is%20the%20beginning%20of

National Geographic Society. (2022a, May 20). *Greek city-states.* National Geographic Society. https://education.nationalgeographic.org/resource/greek-city-states/

National Geographic Society. (2022b, May 20). *Philip II of Macedon.* National Geographic

Society. https://education.nationalgeographic.org/resource/philip-ii-macedon/

National Geographic Society. (2022c, May 20). *The Peloponnesian War*. National Geographic Society. https://education.nationalgeographic.org/resource/peloponnesian-war/

National Geographic Society. (2022d, September 28). *Key components of civilization*. National Geographic. https://education.nationalgeographic.org/resource/key-components-civilization/

Noonan, M. (2023). *Athens vs. Sparta in Ancient Greece*. Study.com. https://study.com/learn/lesson/athens-sparta-differences-life.html#:~:text=Athens%20was%20a%20democratic%20state

O'Connor, J. J., & Robertson, E. F. (2020). *Hypatia of Alexandria*. Maths History. https://mathshistory.st-andrews.ac.uk/Biographies/Hypatia/

orwell1627. (2013, June 30). *Aristotle's purpose of life*. The Great Conversation. https://orwell1627.wordpress.com/2013/06/30/aristotles-purpose-of-life/

Peloponnesian War timeline. (n.d.). World History. https://www.worldhistory.org/timeline/Peloponnesian_War/

Piper, G. (2020, June 9). *After Alexander: The wars of Succession*. Exploring History. https://medium.com/exploring-history/after-alexander-the-wars-of-succession-ecf843c949ca

Rappe, K. (n.d.). *The Greco-Bactrian Mirage: Reconstructing a history Hellenistic Bactria*. Retrieved September 13, 2023, from https://uwarchive.files.wordpress.com/2010/12/kirk-rappe.pdf

Reimer, M. J., & Mackie, J. A. (2019). Alexandria.*Encyclopædia Britannica*. https://www.britannica.com/place/Alexandria-Egypt

Roberts, C. (2023). *Mycenaean civilization*. Study.com. https://study.com/learn/lesson/mycenaean-civilization-social-structure.html#:~:text=The%20Mycenaeans%20flourished%20c.

Roman legionary, Macedonian phalanx, or Spartan hoplite: Which was the better ancient warrior? (2023). History Skills. https://www.historyskills.com/classroom/ancient-history/legion-vs-phalanx-vs-hoplite/

Roos, D. (2019, September 9). *How Alexander the Great conquered the Persian Empire*. HISTORY. https://www.history.com/news/alexander-the-great-defeat-persian-empire

Ryder, M., & Salim, M. (2012). A Middle Eastern vision of progress. *World Pumps*, *2012*(5), 28–31. https://doi.org/10.1016/s0262-1762(12)70128-1

Schools of philosophy in antiquity: Cynics, Epicureans & Stoics. (2023). Study.com.

https://study.com/academy/lesson/schools-of-philosophy-in-antiquity-cynics-epicureans-stoics.html

Schroeder, S. (2017). *The Roman Republic.* Khan Academy. https://www.khanacademy.org/humanities/world-history/ancient-medieval/roman-empire/a/roman-republic

Shewey, D. A. (2004, June 2). *Athenian ambitions & the Delian League.* Western Oregon University. https://wou.edu/history/files/2015/08/David-Shewey.pdf

Shields, C. (2008, September 25). *Aristotle.* Stanford Encyclopedia of Philosophy. https://plato.stanford.edu/entries/aristotle/

Simonin, A. (2011, April 28). *Indo-Greek.* World History Encyclopedia. https://www.worldhistory.org/Indo-Greek/

Smith, P. S. (2019, September 30). *Parthia: Rome's ablest competitor.* World History Encyclopedia. https://www.worldhistory.org/article/1445/parthia-romes-ablest-competitor/

Smith, R. (2017). *Aristotle's logic.* Stanford Encyclopedia of Philosophy. https://plato.stanford.edu/entries/aristotle-logic/

Stamatios, D. (2023, February 5). *Greco-Bactrian Kingdom.* Trenfo. https://www.trenfo.com/en/history/civilizations/greco-bactrian-kingdom

Standjofski, A. (2022, October 20). *What happened during the trial of Socrates?*

TheCollector. https://www.thecollec-
tor.com/the-famous-trial-of-socrates/

Stirn, M. (2022, October 3). Unearthing everyday life at an ancient site in Greece. *The
New York Times.* https://www.ny-
times.com/2022/10/03/travel/iklaina-
archaeology-greece.html

Struck, P. (2000). *The Trojan War.* University
of Pennsylvania. https://www2.classics.up-
enn.edu/myth/php/homer/index.php?page
=trojan

Tai Engen, D. (2019). *The economy of Ancient
Greece.* Eh.net. https://eh.net/encyclope-
dia/the-economy-of-ancient-greece/

Tang, W. (2019, September 19). *The comprehensive Greek islands travel guide.* Going
Awesome Places. https://goingawesome-
places.com/the-comprehensive-greek-
islands-travel-guide/

The dark side of Alexander the Great. (2022,
September 24). Hellenistic History.
https://www.hellenistichis-
tory.com/2022/09/06/the-dark-side-of-
alexander-the-great/

*The development of Archaic, Classical, and Hel-
lenistic sculpture compared to Medieval,
Renaissance, and Baroque.* (n.d.). Google
Arts & Culture. https://artsandcul-
ture.google.com/usergallery/the-
development-of-archaic-classical-and-hel-
lenistic-sculpture-compared-to-medieval-
renaissance-and-baroque/swIyh2aIVVDXJg

The Editors of Encyclopaedia Britannica.
(2017a, December 11). *polis.* Encyclopaedia

Britannica. https://www.britan-
nica.com/topic/polis

The Editors of Encyclopaedia Britannica.
(2017b, December 15). *Academy*. Encyclopedia Britannica.
https://www.britannica.com/topic/Acad-
emy-ancient-academy-Athens-Greece

The Editors of Encyclopaedia Britannica.
(2018). Minos. *Encyclopædia Britannica*.
https://www.britannica.com/topic/Minos

The Editors of Encyclopaedia Britannica.
(2019a). Brasidas. *Encyclopædia Britannica*.
https://www.britannica.com/biog-
raphy/Brasidas

The Editors of Encyclopaedia Britannica.
(2019b). Linear A and Linear B. *Encyclopædia Britannica*.
https://www.britannica.com/topic/Linear-
A

The Editors of Encyclopaedia Britannica.
(2019c). Trojan War. *Encyclopædia Britannica*.
https://www.britannica.com/event/Trojan-
War

The Editors of Encyclopaedia Britannica. (2020,
April 3). *Cleon*. Encyclopedia Britannica.
https://www.britannica.com/biog-
raphy/Cleon-Athenian-politician

The Editors of Encyclopaedia Britannica. (2021,
April 29). *Achievements and decline of the
Hellenistic Age*. Encyclopaedia Britannica.
https://www.britannica.com/sum-
mary/Hellenistic-Age

The Editors of Encyclopædia Britannica. (2009, April 1). *Minoan*. Encyclopedia Britannica. https://www.britannica.com/topic/Minoan

The Editors of Encyclopædia Britannica. (2015). Delian League. *Encyclopædia Britannica.* https://www.britannica.com/topic/Delian-League

The Editors of Encyclopædia Britannica. (2018a). Greco-Persian Wars. *Encyclopædia Britannica.* https://www.britannica.com/event/Greco-Persian-Wars

The Editors of Encyclopædia Britannica. (2018b). Peloponnesian War. *Encyclopædia Britannica.* https://www.britannica.com/event/Peloponnesian-War

The Editors of Encyclopædia Britannica. (2019). Aristotle - Political theory. *Encyclopædia Britannica.* https://www.britannica.com/biography/Aristotle/Political-theory

The Editors of Encyclopædia Britannica. (2020a, August 28). *Alexander the Great's achievements*. Encyclopedia Britannica. https://www.britannica.com/summary/Alexander-the-Greats-Achievements

The Editors of Encyclopædia Britannica. (2020b). League of Corinth | Facts, History, & Definition | Britannica. *Encyclopædia Britannica.* https://www.britannica.com/topic/League-of-Corinth

The Editors of Encyclopædia Britannica. (2021a, April 21). *Parthia*. Encyclopedia Britannica. https://www.britannica.com/place/Parthia

The Editors of Encyclopædia Britannica.
(2021b, April 29). *Explore the military
campaigns of Alexander the Great.* Encyclopedia Britannica.
https://www.britannica.com/summary/Al-
exander-the-Great

The Editors of Encyclopædia Britannica. (2023,
February 27). *Spear.* Encyclopedia Britannica.
https://www.britannica.com/technol-
ogy/spear-weapon#ref186595

The Editors of Encyclopedia Britannica. (2018).
Phidias. *Encyclopædia Britannica.*
https://www.britannica.com/biog-
raphy/Phidias

The Editors of the Encyclopaedia Britannica.
(1998, July 20). *Archilochus.* Encyclopedia
Britannica. https://www.britannica.com/bi-
ography/Archilochus-Greek-author

The Editors of the Encyclopaedia Britannica.
(2021, August 30). *Antigonid dynasty.* Encyclopaedia Britannica.
https://www.britannica.com/topic/Antigo-
nid-dynasty

*The great debate: Who would win if the Roman
legions fought Macedonian phalanxes?*
(2023). History Skills. https://www.histo-
ryskills.com/classroom/ancient-
history/legion-vs-phalanx/

The Greek polis. (2017). Khan Academy.
https://www.khanacademy.org/humani-
ties/world-history/ancient-

medieval/classical-greece/a/the-greek-po-
lis#:~:text=The%20rise%20of%20the%20p
olis

The military revolution: What were Philip II's reforms of the Macedonian military and how revolutionary were they? (n.d.). https://www.ed.ac.uk/files/at-oms/files/the_military_revolution_-_what_were_philip_iis_re-forms_of_the_macedonian_military_and_how_revolutionary_were_they.pdf

The Phaistos Disc. (2022, April 19). Heraklion Archaeological Museum. https://www.hera-klionmuseum.gr/en/exhibit/the-phaistos-disc/#:~:text=The%20Phais-tos%20Disc%20is%20one

Theory of Forms. (n.d.). Saylor Academy. https://learn.say-lor.org/mod/book/tool/print/index.php?id=30538

Tomb of Leonidas. (2016, January 9). Dodeka. http://grecorama.com/en/tomb-of-leoni-das/

Townsend Vermeule, E. D., & Hood, M. S. F. (1999, July 6). *Aegean civilizations.* Ency-clopedia Britannica. https://www.britannica.com/topic/Aegean-civilization

Trelawny-Cassity, L. (n.d.). *Plato: The Acad-emy.* Internet Encyclopedia of Philosophy. https://iep.utm.edu/plato-academy/

Tronson, A. (1984). Satyrus the Peripatetic and the Marriages of Philip II. *The Journal of*

Hellenic Studies, 104, 116–126.
https://doi.org/10.2307/630283

Tsagalis, Christos C. (2020). The Homeric question: a historical sketch. *Yearbook of Ancient Greek Epic Online, 4*(1), 122–162. https://doi.org/10.1163/24688487-00401006

Turner, W. (1903). *Chapter IX: Plato.* History of Philosophy. https://maritain.nd.edu/jmc/etext/hop09.htm

Tyldesley, J. (2019). Cleopatra. *Encyclopædia Britannica.* https://www.britannica.com/biography/Cleopatra-queen-of-Egypt

Vanderpool, E., & Ehrlich, B. (2018). Athens. *Encyclopædia Britannica.* https://www.britannica.com/place/Athens

Virgil. (2019). *Virgil: The Aeneid, Book II.* Poetry in Translation. https://www.poetryintranslation.com/PITBR/Latin/VirgilAeneidII.php

Volkmann, H. (2019a, November 12). *Antigonus.* Encyclopedia Britannica. https://www.britannica.com/biography/Antigonus-I-Monophthalmus

Volkmann, H. (2019b, November 12). *Antigonus II Gonatas.* Encyclopedia Britannica. https://www.britannica.com/biography/Antigonus-II-Gonatas

Walbank, F. W. (1951). The problem of Greek nationality. *Phoenix, 5*(2), 41. https://doi.org/10.2307/1086119

Walbank, F. W. (2018). Alexander the Great. *Encyclopædia Britannica.* https://www.britannica.com/biography/Alexander-the-Great

Wasson, D. (2016, September 29). *Ptolemaic Dynasty.* World History Encyclopedia. https://www.worldhistory.org/Ptolemaic_Dynasty/

Wasson, D. L. (2014, July 31). *Philip II of Macedon.* World History Encyclopedia. https://www.worldhistory.org/Philip_II_of_Macedon/

What did they wear in Ancient Greece? Mycenaean attire. (n.d.). National Clothing. https://nationalclothing.org/europe/42-greece/579-what-did-they-wear-in-ancient-greece-mycenaean-attire.html

Whelan, E. (2020, September 8). *The Age of Homer, or the Dark Ages (12th-9th century).* Classical Wisdom Weekly. https://classicalwisdom.com/culture/history/the-age-of-homer-or-the-dark-ages-12th-9th-century/

Wilburn, H. (2020). *An introduction to Aristotle's metaphysics.* Philosophical Thought. https://open.library.okstate.edu/introphilosophy/chapter/_unknown_/

Williams, J. K. (2008, February 12). *Athens - birthplace of democracy.* New York Post. https://nypost.com/2008/02/12/athens-birthplace-of-democracy/

Williams, R. (2019, August 6). *Macedonian combined arms warfare.* Medium.

https://medium.com/@robert.f.williams/the-macedonian-army-exhibited-a-tactical-brilliance-that-set-a-precedent-in-the-employment-of-9f8548657045

Woerner, J. (2022). *What was the Delian League?* Study.com. https://study.com/learn/lesson/the-delian-league.html#:~:text=The%20Delian%20League%20was%20created

Woodard, T. M., & Taplin, O. (2018). Sophocles. *Encyclopædia Britannica*. https://www.britannica.com/biography/Sophocles

Image References

Atlantios. (2018). Spartan, private, statuette image. In *Photograph*. [Image.] https://pixabay.com/photos/spartan-private-statuette-3082537/

bigfoot. (2013). Fresco, bull, Palace of knossos image. In *Photograph*. [Image.] https://pixabay.com/photos/fresco-bull-palace-of-knossos-111056/

brianneises. (2015). Trojan horse, Troy, Trojan image. In *Photograph*. [Image.] https://pixabay.com/photos/trojan-horse-troy-trojan-horse-607574/

DiscoverMacedonia. (2018). Water, nature, river image. In *Photograph*. [Image.] https://pixabay.com/photos/water-nature-river-travel-mountain-3133678/

ExplorerBob. (2017). Statue, Philip of Macedon, Skopje image. In *Photograph*. [Image.] https://pixabay.com/photos/statue-philip-of-macedon-skopje-2540966/

fietzfotos. (2019). Crete, Greece, amphitheater image. In *Photograph*. [Image.] https://pixabay.com/photos/crete-greece-amphitheater-ancient-4217004/

flutie8211. (2023). Ai generated Alexander the great king royalty-free stock illustration. In *Photograph*. [Image.] https://pixabay.com/illustrations/ai-generated-alexander-the-great-8222225/

GDJ. (2021). The Death Of Socrates Socrates painting royalty-free vector graphic. In *Photograph*. [Image.] https://pixabay.com/vectors/the-death-of-socrates-socrates-6471743/

Gina_Janosch. (2016). Mycenae, Lions tomb, wall image. In *Photograph*. [Image.] https://pixabay.com/photos/mycenae-lions-tomb-wall-1350376/

Hans. (2016). Italy Alps Alpine region royalty-free stock illustration. In *Photograph*. [Image.] https://pixabay.com/illustrations/italy-alps-alpine-region-map-1804893/

HeikoAL. (2017). Crete, museum, historical image. In *Photograph*. [Image.] https://pixabay.com/photos/crete-museum-historical-old-minoan-2391755/

rickytolt186. (2022). Bucephalus, the war of the heavenly horses, Ferghana horse image. In *Photograph*. [Image.] https://pixabay.com/photos/bucephalus-6952339/

Louis le Grand. (2007) Marble bust of Cleopatra VII of Egypt from ca. 40-30 BC. marked as public domain, details on Wikimedia Commons: https://commons.wikimedia.org/wiki/Template:PD-old [Image.] https://commons.wikimedia.org/wiki/File:Kleopatra-VII.-Altes-Museum-Berlin1.jpg

Rita E. (2017). Sea, Aegean sea, outlook image. In *Photograph*. [Image.] https://pixabay.com/photos/sea-aegean-sea-outlook-neipori-2729955/

stux. (2013). Ancient, temple, nature image. In *Photograph*. [Image.] https://pixabay.com/photos/ancient-temple-ruin-corinthian-170183/

symvol. (2014). London, British museum, Ancient Greece image. In *Photograph*. [Image.] https://pixabay.com/photos/london-british-museum-ancient-greece-244263/

user32212. (2017). Acropolis, Parthenon, ancient image. In *Photograph*. [Image.] https://pixabay.com/photos/acropolis-parthenon-ancient-columns-2047093/

VIVIANE6276. (2019). Homer, Odyssey, Ancient Greece image. In *Photograph*. [Image.] https://pixabay.com/photos/homer-odyssey-ancient-greece-a%C3%A8de-4570409/

Vlachos, N. (2022). A statue of a man riding a horse.
In *Photograph*. [Image.]
https://unsplash.com/photos/nfSsyAkYgcs
wpaczocha. (2017). Terrace cultivation, terrace,
Greece image. In *Photograph*. [Image.]
https://pixabay.com/photos/terrace-cultiva-
tion-terrace-greece-2745920/